I0167415

Remembering my Creator since my youth

David Anderson

Scripture Truth Publications

Revised and reprinted from a series entitled "Creation" in "Scripture Truth" magazine, Volumes 56-58, 2009-14.
First edition August 2014
ISBN: 978-0-901860-93-4 (paperback)
Copyright © 2014 David Anderson and Scripture Truth Publications
A publication of Scripture Truth

Introduction

I have always believed in God. Since early childhood, I have always known that He created all things through His Son, Jesus Christ, my Lord and Saviour. As a child, I attended St. Lawrence Sunday School, Byker, Newcastle upon Tyne (yes, Byker made notorious by the TV programme 'Byker Grove'!). There I was taught that the Word of God is true in its entirety, that is, *from its very beginning* (compare Psalm 119:160, NKJV with KJV). Although I cannot remember a date/time for my conversion, the reality is that I *do* believe in Jesus Christ, the Son of God. Therefore, I *am* saved (compare John 3:16-18).

Since my mid-teens, I have been involved with children's summer camps held at Fenham Farm, Beal, Northumberland. The campsite is situated on the Fenham Bay shoreline overlooking Holy Island. Fenham Christian Camps appropriately use Ecclesiastes 12:1 (NKJV), "Remember now your Creator in the days of your youth", in its logo. This book is the outcome of my lifelong application of this verse, as its title, "Remembering my Creator since my youth", implies. I am one of just a few campers who have ever got up early enough to contemplate the raw beauty of creation in the pre-dawn colours of the sunrise from behind Holy Island. And, I think, I am unique among them in that I have also experienced this beauty in the long dawn of mid-summer day, when the sun rises over the Snook of Holy Island!

WHY IS THIS BOOK SO IMPORTANT?

Some readers will know me as a scientist. But this book is *not* primarily about the "science versus the Bible" debate, important as that is with respect to the truths of the Gospel. However, I do briefly discuss this issue, as a postscript, in Part 6 of this book. It is about the more important matter of what the Bible, the *Word of God*, teaches about creation; and why we believers must hold to this doctrine in an increasingly materialistic and secular world, with its aggressive and hostile atheists. "Science, at its best, is only relative truth for today and may be proved wrong tomorrow; but Scripture is absolute truth which abides forever." Words to this effect were once said to me by the late J. S. Blackburn, who, like myself, started his professional life as an analytical chemist; and who was a former editor of *Scripture Truth* magazine. As a teenager I personally experienced the penetrating effect of God's Word – as a discerner of the thoughts and intentions of the heart (Hebrews 4:12). After a career of over forty years as a practising chemist in the Active Pharmaceutical Ingredients' industry, with its exacting science, and now as a 'wise OAP', I remain as convinced as then of the accuracy and inerrancy of the Bible. The Scriptures are the only reliable source of truth about all matters of the Christian faith, including those relating to the origins of the universe and the world; and to life itself. Moreover, Creation is a bedrock under the whole of Bible truth. To

4

deny, question, or even modify, the Genesis account is to challenge the truth of God, "Can it really be true what God said?" (Compare Genesis 3:1, AMP).

Hebrews 11:3 informs us it is *by faith* that Christians understand that the universe was created by the word of God. So what *must* I believe about creation? This *apologia* for the biblical view attempts to answer that crucial question.

Acknowledgements

The majority of this book first appeared as a series of articles in *Scripture Truth* magazine (July 2009-April 2014). I am indebted to Theo Balderston for all his editorial work. I thank Ernie Brown for proof-reading the book. My daughter, Sheila, also helped in the reviews. Finally, I acknowledge the constant support of my wife, Gillian, who is a true "help meet for" me.

Infinity

Clever people made the car
and invented the PC:
Someone greater, greater far,
made the universe, and me.

Could the car occur by chance?
Or PCs by accident?
Far, far less did happenstance
this huge universe invent.

Stars and universe declare,
in their vast immensity,
that the God whose work they are,
far, far greater is than they,

infinite in power and mind.
Greater the infinity
that for Christ a cross defined,
One for one, God's Son for me.

THEO BALDERSTON

REMEMBERING MY CREATOR SINCE MY YOUTH

Contents

Part 1
The
Fundamentals

Chapter 1
Is it necessary to believe in biblical creation?

WHAT DOES THE SCRIPTURE SAY?

Scripture has very much to say about creation. It runs like bedrock under the Bible from Genesis to Revelation. Throughout it we find, as we would expect, the basic truths about God and creation, and Christ and creation. But, perhaps less familiarly, we also find that the Gospel and creation are intrinsically related, as are Christian doctrine and creation, "things to come" and creation, and judgment and creation. These six topics are discussed in this chapter.

GOD AND CREATION

1 Corinthians 8:6 is almost a statement of faith about creation. "For us [Christian believers] there is one God, the Father, from whom are all things and for whom we exist, and one Lord, Jesus Christ, through whom are all things and through whom we exist." God is the Source of everything, our omniscient Creator, our Maker who framed and made the world we live in and gave all animals and human beings their natural life. The

following examples illustrate how this truth runs through the Scriptures:

- God is the self-existent and unchanging One, who declares "I am he" in Deuteronomy 32:39; Isaiah 41:4, 43:10 & 25, 46:4, 48:12 & 51:12. The N.Tr. of Psalm 102:27 (quoted in Hebrews 1:12) calls Him "the Same" and its footnote comments, "a name of God, 'The existing One, who does not change' ...." God is eternal, infinite, immutable and transcendent, outside of all of His creation.

- God the Creator brought the universe, man and everything else that has created being, into existence. Hebrew has a word mainly reserved for this divine act: the verb 'created' occurs, for example, in Genesis 1:1, 21, 27 & 2:3-4; Isaiah 40:26 & 45:18; Malachi 2:10. Its noun 'creator' occurs in Ecclesiastes 12:1 & Isaiah 40: 28. So does the Greek; and this word occurs, for example, as 'created' in Mark 13:19; Revelation 4:11 & 10:6, and 'creator' in Romans 1:25 & 1 Peter 4:19.

- God made, fashioned (and maintains) all that He brought into existence. He did not leave the fashioning of it to chance! Various more general words in Scripture frequently speak of this. For example: Psalm 33:6, 74:17, 94:9 & 95:6; Zechariah 12:1; Acts 14:15-17, 17:24 & 26; Revelation 14:7.

- God decreed and laid the foundations of the earth, as many Scriptures confirm. For example, Job 38:4; Psalm 104:5; Proverbs 8:29; Isaiah 51:13.

- God is the One on whom all creatures rely for life, practical care and protection. See: Psalms 36:5-9, 104:27 & 145:15-16; Isaiah 40:26-31; Acts 14:15, 17:24 & 26.

- God is the Judge, who demands an answer from all of His creatures. Reference: Genesis 14:19; Romans 14:11-12 (quoting from Isaiah 45:22-23); Revelation 20:12.

'Creator' is a fundamental title of God in Scripture. Essential attributes of His nature and character are displayed in His creatorial actions. They include:

- His eternal nature, Psalm 90:1-2; Revelation 4:8 & 11.
- His omniscience and His omnipotence, Job 38, 42:1-2; Psalm 33:6 & 9; Isaiah 40:12-14 & 25-28.
- His transcendence, Job 37:14-23; Psalm 97:9.
- His sovereignty, Psalm 135:5-7.
- His righteousness, Psalms 36:6 & 97:6.
- His fullness of wisdom and mercy, Psalm 136:5 (KJV).
- His care for His people, Psalm 121:1-2.

CHRIST AND CREATION

Genesis 1:1 opens with the words, "In the beginning God created the heavens and the earth." But the word translated "God" is *Elohim*, which is a Hebrew plural (in fact denoting more than two). So, also in verse 26, it is *Elohim* who said, "Let us make man in our image, after our likeness." The whole Godhead was involved in the work of creation (Ephesians 3:9). But the New Testament teaches that the Son, the Lord Jesus Christ, was the primary Agent of the Godhead in this work. Each of the three great New-Testament passages delineating the glories of His Person says this.

John 1:3 says concerning "the Word" that, "All things were made through him; and without him was not anything made." "The Word", essentially God and yet a distinct Personality in God, is the One Who alone is able to fully declare God (1:1, 2 & 18). "The Word" first expressed God *in creation.* (Psalm 19:1-4 & Romans 1:19-20 confirm that creation is a declaration of God.) When John 3:35 tell us that, "The Father loves the Son and has given all things into his hand", these "all things" include the work of creation, as well the works of redemption and judgment. Whatever the Father wills, the Son is able to carry out to completion.

Hebrews 1 presents the greatness of the Son. Verses 1-2 underline the greatness of God speaking "in Son" (verse 2, N.Tr.), and no longer in the Old Testament prophets, by identifying the Son as the One "through whom also [God] made the worlds" (NKJV). Verse 3 further states that the Son continuously upholds "the universe by the word of his power" – the same "word" by which He brought creation into existence. Then verses 10-12 state that when the earth and the heavens have served God's purpose, "the Son" will fold them up like a garment. But *He* remains eternally "the Same" (verse 12, N.Tr.).

Colossians 1:15-17 begins a flowing description of the glories of the Lord Jesus Christ by declaring His majesty as Creator. He is the Son (compare verse 13), and these verses (especially verse 17) show His transcendence, as existing before, above and beyond creation, altogether outside of it.

- When verse 15 describes Him as "the firstborn of all creation", "firstborn" carries the non-literal sense of "status in relation to others" (compare Psalm 89:27 & Jeremiah 31:9), and does not contradict verse 17. "Firstborn" sets Him high above and over all of it as its Creator.

- The "by him" at the start of verse 16 should read "in the power of whose person" (N.Tr. footnote). The footnote continues, "He was the one whose intrinsic power characterised the creation. It exists as his creature", which implies the Lord's intrinsic ability to design the creation. He is its Author and its Cause.

- The rest of verse 16 declares His involvement in every aspect of creating – "the things in the heavens and the things upon the earth, the visible and the invisible, whether thrones or lordships or principalities, or authorities" (N.Tr.).

- The last clause of verse 16 should read, "all things have been created through him and unto him" (RV). "Through him" defines Christ as God's Agent in the every act of creating. "Unto him" signifies that He is the ultimate reason for creation – its goal – and that *He* answers the question, "Why is there a creation?" See further footnotes in N.Tr. to verse 16.

- Verse 17 (RV) states that "in him all things consist" and echoes the truths of Hebrews 1:3 & 10-12.

THE GOSPEL AND CREATION

Why does the Gospel need to be proclaimed? Because mankind *should, and are able to,* know God through His creation, and yet they have not worshipped Him as God. This is how Paul's great exposition of the Gospel in Romans opens. He says God's wrath is deservedly revealed against all men's ungodliness and unrighteousness (1:18). Why? Because "what can be known about God is plain to them, because God has shown it to them. For his invisible attributes, namely, his eternal power and divine nature, have been clearly perceived, ever since the creation of the world, in the things that have been made. So they are without excuse" (1:19-20).

17

People choose to ignore God their Creator; and have "exchanged the truth about God for a lie and worshipped and served the creature rather than the Creator" (1:21-23 & 25). Both conscience and commandment (2:15 & 23) witness to the fact that "all [of mankind] are under sin. ... For all have sinned and fall short of the glory of God" (3:9 & 23). But primarily it is the testimony of creation that proves the case against them. We should confidently base our proclamation of the Gospel on this analysis. Paul did. In Lystra, where the people wished to turn Barnabas and himself into gods, he immediately proclaimed their Creator, "We bring you good news, that you should turn from these vain things to a living God, who made the heaven and the earth and the sea and all that is in them" (Acts 14:15). He did this again in Athens when he was provoked by the sight of all their idols (Acts 17:16 & 22-31). In both places he preached the obligation of every human being to acknowledge and repent towards the Creator.

NEW-TESTAMENT DOCTRINE AND CREATION

Some people think that since creation comes at the beginning of the Old Testament, they can be 'New Testament Christians' whilst shelving the question of the factual accuracy of the Genesis account. If they think this, they are not 'New Testament Christians', for the Creatorship of God, even in its details (Genesis 1-3), is fundamental to many other vital matters of Christian faith and conduct. For example:

- the entrance into the world of sin and death, Romans 5:12

- the doctrine concerning all suffering in the world and its solution, Romans 8:19-22

- bodily resurrection, 1 Corinthians 15:20-58
- marriage, Mark 10:2-12
- headship, 1 Corinthians 11:2-16 & 1 Timothy 2:8-15
- God's providential care, Matthew 6:26-30 & 1 Timothy 4:3-5.

By "wobbling" on the matter of creation, we are in grave danger of appearing/seeming to undermine the Bible's teaching, and of consequently challenging its authority, on these other basics too! And, because these are vital matters, I'll flesh them out in more detail in Chapter 4.

CREATION AND "THINGS TO COME"

Many Old Testament writers demonstrate Israel's specific appreciation, as God's chosen people, that He is their Creator. For example, "Know that the LORD, he is God! It is he who made us, and we are his; we are his people, and the sheep of his pasture" (Psalm 100:3). The immeasurable vastness and fixed order of the creation guarantees Israel's future new covenant blessings (Jeremiah 31:35-37). All the prophets project forward to the coming kingdom of Messiah, which will witness a restoration of God's original creatorial purpose. Of many Scriptures that show this, perhaps the climax of the books of Psalms does it best. Psalm 150:6 exclaims, "Let everything that has breath [that is, every living creature which breathes][1] praise the LORD!" Psalm 148 enjoins all created beings and creation itself to praise Him. Psalm 8, which announces the prophetic intent of the Psalms, starts with a contemplation of Adam's original dominion over God's creation before the Fall, but points forward to the millennial reign of the true "Son of man" who will bring harmony back into creation (see verses 4-8 with Hebrews 2:5-9). Then the lion and lamb will lie down together; a revitalised earth will give of its bounty and the desert blossom as a rose; and there will be peace and security for mankind, when each sits under his vine and none makes him afraid. See Isaiah 32:17-18; 35:1 (NKJV); 65:25; Micah 4:4.

The New Testament describes "the world to come" more fully. The "God who created all things" has made known to us the secret of His will, namely, His purpose in the fullness of times to head up all things in Christ, both things in heaven and things on earth (Ephesians 1:9, 10 & 22; 3:9, N.Tr.). God's right to ultimate and eternal glory from His creation is succinctly summarised in Revelation 4:11, "Worthy are you, our Lord and God, to receive glory and honour and power, for you created all things, and by your will they existed and were created." And when Christ has, by purchase, been able to take the title deeds to the kingdom (5:7), causing the redeemed in heaven to exclaim in verse 12, "Worthy is the Lamb who was slain, to receive power …", *then* John hears "every creature in heaven and on earth and under the earth and in the sea, and all that is in them, saying, 'To him who sits on the throne and to the Lamb be blessing and honour and glory and might forever and ever'" (5:13).

JUDGMENT AND CREATION

As already stated, Romans 1:19-20 indicts men before the judgment of God for having flouted the witness of creation. Their wilful neglect of God has *already* resulted in His governmental judgment on them, in which He has given them over to the depravity of their sinful ways (1:21-28). Verse 32 concludes that they have qualified themselves for the *coming* judgment of God, and 2:1-16 elaborates on this.

Adam and Eve failed in the simple test of obedience to their Creator. But under the Gospel everyone is also placed under the requirement of obedience – the obedience of *faith*. This is the command of the eternal God (Romans 1:5, 6:17 & 16:26). But "faith comes by hearing" (10:17) and so in 10:18 Paul asks (rhetorically) whether all have, in fact, heard? Quoting Psalm 19:4, that great "gospel of creation in song", he replies, "Indeed they have, for 'their voice has gone out to all the earth, and their words to the ends of the world.'" Creation witnesses against them if they claim not to have heard! And yet, God is reluctant to judge. Even in the last hour, just before the awful seven bowls of God's wrath are poured out upon earth, He sends his messenger to reiterate the message of creation. "Then I saw another angel flying directly overhead, with an eternal gospel to proclaim to those who dwell on earth, to every nation and tribe and language and people. And he said with a loud voice, 'Fear God and give him glory, because the hour of his judgment has come, and worship him who made heaven and earth, the sea and the springs of water'" (Revelation 14:6-7).

A SCRIPTURAL DOXOLOGY TO THE CREATOR

"Oh, the depth of the riches and wisdom and knowledge of God! How unsearchable are his judgments and how inscrutable his ways! 'For who has known the mind of the Lord, or who has been his counsellor?' 'Or who has given a gift to him that he might be repaid?' For from him and through him and to him are all things. To him be glory forever. Amen" (Romans 11:33-36).

REMEMBERING MY CREATOR SINCE MY YOUTH

Chapter 2
What happened at Creation?

GENESIS 1-2

In Chapter 1, I discussed the Scriptural doctrines about creation as made clear in the New Testament. I concluded that because creation underpins many of its major doctrines, Divine creation as revealed in Genesis is not an option for the Christian! This chapter therefore goes back to Genesis and answers the question, "What is God saying to us in the original account of creation?"

GENESIS 1:1 IS GOD'S POSITION STATEMENT ABOUT HIS CREATION

"In the beginning, God created the heavens and the earth" are the very first words of Scripture. Ten English words translate the seven original Hebrew words. In that sense they are a *complete statement* about creation. The remainder of the Genesis account (and all other teaching on creation throughout Scripture) simply elaborates this emphatic statement.

The Hebrew word for "God" is *Elohim*, which is a plural noun (in fact denoting more than two). He is the eternal, almighty, majestic, omnipotent, supreme,

23

absolute, self-existing One. In Genesis 1 we are told that He created (a singular verb) the whole realm of space (the heavens) and the earth by calling them into existence from nothing. The Hebrew text uses the special word, *bara*, for 'to create' to convey the meaning 'creation out of nothing'. As Romans 4:17 states, "God ... calls into existence the things that do not exist." Hebrews 11:3 adds, "By faith we understand that the universe was created by the word of God, so that what is seen was not made out of things that are visible."

But God also created time – so we may paraphrase verse 1 as "when God created, time started". In verse 2 the specific activity of the Spirit is mentioned; and the words "in the beginning" are also the opening words of John's Gospel, where the New Testament revelation is that it was the Word (that is, the Son) who created all things (John 1:1-3). The whole Godhead was thus involved in creation.

The focus of these opening two verses is the earth. Verse 2 goes on to describe its initial condition as being "without form and void", that is, both unformed and uninhabited. The best analogy that we can use here about the Creator is that He is like a potter,[1] who first of all makes the shapeless clay before moulding it into the shape(s) he has in mind. Most importantly, Isaiah explains that His design intent was not to leave the earth in that condition but to make it suitable for mankind. "The LORD, who created the heavens (he is God!), who formed the earth and made it (he established it; he did not create it empty,[2] he formed it to be inhabited!): 'I am the Lord, and there is no other'" (45:18). Genesis 1:2 also states that darkness was over the face of the deep with the Spirit of God hovering over the waters. The immediate effect of the Spirit's movements was the creation of light (Genesis 1:3-5). God created both the darkness and the light (Isaiah 45:7). He deliberately worked this way and separated [that is, provided a distinction between] the two. In 2 Corinthians 4:6 (N.Tr.), He is described as, "the God who spoke that out of darkness light should shine". And so the first day ends this way – the light (morning) follows the darkness (evening).

DAY ONE: THE FUNDAMENTALS, VERSES 1-5

On the first day of creation, God created:

- Time, "in the beginning" – the clock started to tick.
- The universe, "the heavens and the earth". Or to express it another way:
  - "the heavens" to us is the vastness of outer space
  - "the earth" is planet earth, which consists of all materials. But, notice the emphasis on water in the following verses.
- Energy, "the light", a fundamental for life.

From these created things, God set about to structure/fashion/form His creation and to fill the earth to make it habitable by man, His special object in creation. God could have done everything instantaneously on Day One. But He took five more days to do it, as the recurring words in Genesis 1, "God said .... And it was so", suggest.

DAY TWO: THE "EXPANSE", VERSES 6-8

God spoke, and made an expanse [or, canopy] to divide [separate] the waters around the unformed earth. This canopy is described as a "mist" in 2:6. 2 Peter 3:5-7 describe the unformed earth as surrounded by water and explain the way in which it and the antediluvian world were changed at the Flood. Therefore it is difficult to know (in our postdiluvian world) exactly what this "mist" was, but nowadays the sky is usually regarded as what God named as "heaven" in verse 8. It would seem that the expanse of verse 15 is outer space; but that of verse 20 is the earth's atmosphere. But as verse 16 mentions the stars, the expanse sometimes includes outer space.

DAY THREE: EARTH AND SEAS, VERSES 9-13

God gathered all the waters together to form "seas", and separated them from the dry land ("earth"). He caused all kinds of vegetation – plant life and trees, each with the ability to seed – to come into existence on the land. These were provided as food for animals and man (verses 29-30). Now there was life! Twice over on Day Three, God saw that what He had done was good (verses 10 & 12).

DAY FOUR: SUN AND MOON AND STARS, VERSES 14-19

God appointed light-bearers to regulate life for man by making the sun and the moon (and the planets and the stars). There is an up-front statement of intent: "God said, 'Let there be lights in the expanse of the heavens to separate the day from the night. And let them be for signs and for seasons, and for days and years'" (verse 14). Whilst in some translations, "and the stars" at the end of verse 16 could be read as an add-on or passing comment, the ESV and other translations show the stars to be of equal importance as the sun and the moon, "God made the two great lights – the greater light to rule the day and the lesser light to rule the night – and the stars." As we shall explore in Chapter 5, other Scriptures show the magnitude of God's creatorial actions here on Day Four, when He took the heavens He had made on

Day One and stretched them out as we would do with curtains.

DAY FIVE: POPULATING THE SEAS AND SKIES, VERSES 20-23

God completely filled both of these spheres with all kinds of creatures, both great and small. Verse 21 uses the special word, *bara* ("create"), to describe the making of living things with personality, i.e., conscious life ("every living soul", N.Tr.). God gave abundant life to all. "And God blessed them, saying, 'Be fruitful and multiply and fill the waters in the seas, and let birds multiply on the earth'" (verse 22).

DAY SIX (A): LAND CREATURES, VERSES 24-25

God filled the land with all kinds of land animals and other creatures, again, both great and small – and also those which are now extinct, e.g., dinosaurs. Then God reviewed all His work so far in this first part of Day Six. He "saw that it was good" (verse 25). The world was now ready for man.

DAY SIX (B): MAN, VERSES 26-31

Because God's creation was now ready for man, verse 26 begins "Then God said" (compare "And God said", verses 3, 6, 9, 14, 20 & 24) showing that when God created Adam, He achieved His objective. "And God [now] saw everything that he had made, and behold, it was *very* good [literally, "exceedingly good"] ..." (verse 31). The special word, *bara* ("create"), is used in verse 27 to distinguish man from the rest of the animal creation. Verse 26 informs us that man is above all other created life and that he was the special subject of divine counsel, "Let us make man in our image, after our likeness. And let them have dominion over [all creatures]." Genesis 2:4-7 states that God adopted a special procedure of forming man from the dust of the earth and intimately breathing life into him – different from the animal creation when He spoke life into them. So man became a unique living being. (2:21-23 describe the special way Eve was built out of Adam.)

Being made in God's image and after His likeness means that man is unique. This transcendental nature of man manifests itself in:

1 Rationality – we have minds which are capable of abstract thoughts, reason, originality, design and genius.

2 Volition – we have the capacity to make decisions and choices.

3 Conscience – we make moral choices. Everyone basically knows good from evil.

4 Aestheticism – we appreciate truth and goodness. We possess a sense of beauty and emotion.

> ➤ But, points 1-4 are cumulative – meaning we clearly understand creation to be God's handiwork (see Romans 1:19-20). All conscious life has an inherent sense of their Creator! But we humans also deliberately choose whether to believe this or not!

5 Our spiritual dimension. We are not only body and soul, but also spirit. Therefore anyone can get to know God and worship Him. Adam and Eve's spiritual experiences were of direct communion with God.

6 Representation. In verse 28, God charges them to represent and express Him, the invisible God, to a visible creation. Adam primarily had this dignity and was given dominion over everything in the seas,

in the air, and on the earth. When 2:15 states, "The LORD God took the man and put him in the garden of Eden to work it and keep it", it shows that stewardship/duty is implicit in the idea of human authority over God's creation.

THE CREATION WEEK CULMINATES IN THE SABBATH, 2:1-3

The Spirit of God counts up the days of this first week, using the formula "there was evening and morning,[3] an [or, 'the'] xth day" –and this means *literally* a 24-hour day. For example, Robert Young's literal translation for 1:5 reads, "and God calleth to the light 'Day,' and to the darkness He hath called 'Night;' and there is an evening, and there is a morning – day one."[4] Each day is chronologically sequential as the repeated use of the conjunction "and" to start the sentences shows. Similarly, the conjunction "and" time-connects Genesis 1:1 with all sentences of verses 2-5. In other words, verses 1-5 all describe all God's actions on Day One.

There may be some significance in the fact that, in the original Hebrew, only Genesis 1:31 prefixes the definite article to the day – "*the* sixth day", whereas it is not present in relation to the first five days. The sixth was the culminating day of creation, not least because man was created in it.

1:31 draws attention to everything God had made, "behold, it was very good." His satisfaction was expressed in His rest from work on the seventh day (2:3). He made it a distinct day in the cycle of days that form a week. He blessed it and sanctified it. From the beginning, He established the pattern of life for man – to work for six days and hold a seventh day set apart for God. It is very interesting that, unlike other time measures such as months and years, there seems to be no other reason (either in Scripture or in the history/ experience/science of mankind) for the measurement of seven days or one week. Its importance is stressed in the Decalogue, "Remember the Sabbath day, to keep it holy. Six days you shall labour, and do all your work, but the seventh day is a Sabbath to the LORD your God. On it you shall not do any work, you, or your son, or your daughter, your male servant, or your female servant, or your livestock, or the sojourner who is within your gates. For in six days the LORD made heaven and earth, the sea, and all that is in them, and rested the seventh day. Therefore the LORD blessed the Sabbath day and made it holy" (Exodus 20:8-11 and reiterated in Deuteronomy 5:12-15). The Sabbath became a distinctive sign between Jehovah and the nation of Israel (Exodus 31:12-17). And the Lord Jesus said that the Sabbath was made for man's benefit (Mark 2:27, compare Exodus 23:12).

Genesis 2 opens with a summary statement of creation, which brings to a conclusion the events of the creation week, "Thus the heavens and the earth were finished, and all the host of them. ... So God blessed the seventh day and made it holy, because on it God rested from all his work that he had done in creation" (2:1 & 3). Thus, 2:1-3 more properly belong to the narrative of Genesis 1 and 2:4 starts a new section about Man.

THE GENERATIONS OF THE HEAVENS AND THE EARTH, 2:4-7

Genesis is a history book about the important generations of early mankind (2:4).[5] The remarkable climax of the generations of the heavens and the earth is man (2:7)! God is called Jehovah Elohim ("LORD God") from Genesis chapter 2 verse 4 and through chapter 3, that is, He is the God who forms relationships with men. 2:5-6 reveal that throughout the creation week His thoughts were centred on man. Verse 7 explains how He formed man from the ground and gave him life by breathing into him so that he became a unique living being, who was different to all other creatures and who was given a unique position in God's creation. Then the remainder of Genesis chapter 2 details God's attention to man's welfare and expands on how He provided for mankind. The importance of mankind in creation is also shown in 5:1-2 where their creation is the first-mentioned fact of Adam's genealogy!

GOD'S BLESSING OF MAN, 2:8-25

Unlike 1:1 – 2:3, these verses are not always chronological. They expand upon 1:28, "And God blessed them, and God said to them, 'Be fruitful and multiply and fill the earth ….'". God blessed man by planting the Garden of Eden, as a special environment for man, with food, water and minerals in abundance (2:8-14). Everything in it was there to sustain man, especially the tree of life – so that man could go on living forever (3:22). The tree of the knowledge of good and evil was also there in the midst of the garden, to test man's on-going relationship with the Lord God. The conditions of this relationship were clearly explained to man in verses 16-17. Eden was supplied with a four-headed river so that there was water in abundance. Over and above all of these things, God blessed man by providing woman for him. The Lord God recognized that it was not good for Adam to be alone. He said, "I will make him a helper fit for him" (verse 18). Adam did not find a helpmate for himself in the animal kingdom (verses 19-20). So the Lord God built Eve from Adam's side, and presented her to him as his wife. Adam found in Eve his counterpart, one who was like himself. Thus human relationships were established. "Therefore a man shall leave his father and his mother and hold fast to his wife, and they shall become one flesh" (verse 24), setting forth an eternal reality which awaited New Testament revelation (Ephesians 5:25-32). Human relationships were to be built around the family unit. The intimate relationship of man and wife was based upon their distinctive sexualities (Genesis 1:27). It was good, proper, beneficial and healthy to both of them (2:25).

DOXOLOGY

"Jehovah Elohim is truth; he is the living God, and the king of eternity. ... He hath made the earth by his power, he hath established the world by his wisdom, and hath stretched out the heavens by his understanding" (Jeremiah 10:10 & 12, N.Tr.).

NOTE: WORDS AND THEIR SIGNIFICANCE IN THE GENESIS ACCOUNT

Various Hebrew words are used in Genesis chapters 1-2 to describe God's work in creation. The following is a précis of my research into these words. It is mainly derived from the detailed exposition given in 'Vine's complete expository dictionary of Old and New Testament words'[6]:

1 *Bara* (meaning to create, make, shape, form) in 1:1, 21 & 27; 2:3 & 4. This verb has only God as its subject and it expresses creation out of nothing.

2 *Asah* (meaning to create, do, make, fashion, accomplish) in 1:7, 16, 25-26 & 31; 2:2-4, 18. It is used to describe how God structured and formed His creation.

3 *Yâtsar* (meaning to form, fashion, frame) in 2:7-8 & 19.

4 *Banah* (meaning to build) in 2:22.

The context determines the sense in which any word is used. *Bara* is selectively used for highlighting the special work of creating:

- ➤ the heavens and the earth, 1:1

- ➤ the first living souls, 1:20-21 (N.Tr.)

- ➤ mankind, 1:27.

However:

- *Bara* is also used interchangeably with *asah* in 1:26-27 & 2:4, where its meaning must include the action of forming as well as creating:

  - ▪ "Then God said, 'Let us make [*asah*] man in our image, after our likeness. And let them have dominion over the fish of the sea and over the birds of the heavens and over the livestock and over all the earth and over every creeping thing that creeps on the earth.' So God created [*bara*] man in his own image, in the image of God he created [*bara*] him; male and female he created [*bara*] them" (1:26-27).

  - ▪ "These are the generations of the heavens and the earth when they were created [*bara*], in the day that the LORD God made [*asah*] the earth and the heavens" (2:4).

- In 2:3 (KJV) they are used alongside each other, "And God blessed the seventh day, and sanctified it: because that in it he had rested from all his work which God created [*bara*] and made [*asah*]."

  - ▪ The KJV margin and N.Tr. footnote both give the literal meaning, 'created to make'.

- And 5:1 equates *bara* with *asah*, "When God created [*bara*] man, he made [*asah*] him in the likeness of God."

Chapter 3
What happened after the Creation?

Our experience of everyday life proves that this present creation is a "groaning creation" (Romans 8:22). People criticise God for it. But God didn't create it that way. The creation was "very good" when it left the hand of God. So the question arises, "What happened to change the creation?"

WHAT HAPPENED NEXT?

The world we live in is so different to the one described in Genesis chapters 1 & 2 – the world which God blessed (1:22, 28 & 2:3 with 5:2). Therefore, we must ask, "What happened *after* the Creation?" For, each day from Day Three of the Creation Week, God reviewed what He had made, and "saw that it was good" (1:10, 12, 18, 21 & 25). This reached a climax on the sixth day, when, having made and blessed Man, "God saw everything that He had made, and behold, it was *very* good [literally, "exceedingly good"]" (1:31). Furthermore, Man is again the highlight of the creation in the summary statement about "the generations of the heavens and the earth" (2:4-7).

But we are acutely aware that things must have drastically changed for the worse. So we ask the questions, "How, when and why did this change happen?" For what human heart does not agonise for conditions where there is no more sin, suffering, pain or death? What human spirit does not subconsciously yearn for a state where righteousness reigns/dwells? And what believer does not appreciate that "in this hope we are saved" and is patiently waiting for it (Romans 8:24-25)? Or what part of creation does not exhibit that groaning about which the passage (Romans 8:19-23) speaks?

The subsequent chapters of Genesis reveal why things at the present time are so different from life for Adam and Eve in the Garden of Eden. They record three catastrophic events concerning Man (and creation):

> ➢ the Fall
>
> ➢ the Flood
>
> ➢ the Dispersion.

THE FALL: GENESIS 3

It seems that, soon after creation, Adam disobeyed God and sinned by eating of the fruit of the tree of the knowledge of good and evil, which he had been forbidden to eat (Genesis 2:16-17). Whilst Eve was deceived (Genesis 3:13 & 1 Timothy 2:14), it was Adam, there by her side, who bore the responsibility for their actions. He ate of the fruit of the tree of the knowledge of good and evil in blatant defiance of the command of God (2:17 & 3:6). They had, to this point in their lives, only experienced good. Now they knew evil and were conscious of their sin, expressed by the fact that "they knew they were naked" (3:7). Consequently, they hid themselves from God (3:10). They had died spiritually and the process of mortality began for them, although it was another 900 years or so before they physically died. God's word was true, "for in the day that thou eatest thereof thou shalt surely die" – literally, "dying thou shalt die" (2:17, KJV and margin). And what became true of them became true also of the whole creation over which God had given them dominion. This was shown to them that very same day by God when He made for them garments of skin to clothe them (3:21).

It is so important to see that *this* is why we do not see the creation today as it came from the hand of God, because the Fall of Man is a fundamental in the doctrine of the Gospel. Romans 5:12 teaches that sin and death came through Adam's transgression. That was when both entered into our world. In other words, there was no sin or death in the world that God created *prior to* the Fall! After that, sin spread to all mankind. Cain was conceived and born *after* Adam and Eve had sinned (Genesis 4:1). Romans 5:12 goes on to state that Adam, the progenitor of the human race, passed on his fallen condition to his descendants. (This is reinforced in 1 Corinthians 15:22 where Paul states that it is *in Adam* that all die.) Therefore the Gospel pronounces a guilty verdict on all mankind, "all [people] are under sin" and therefore, "all have sinned and fall short of the glory of God" (Romans 3:9 & 23).

But Adam was also a type of the One who was to come (Romans 5:14). Jesus Christ is the Last Adam, the Head of the redeemed race (those who believe the Gospel). They partake in the spiritual character and heavenly position of their Head and will bear His image (1 Corinthians 15:42-49). But Christ is also the Second Man who was conceived by the direct action of the Holy Spirit upon the Virgin Mary (Luke 1:35). The Second

Man is entirely different to those of Adam's race – He "knew no sin," "He committed no sin," and "in him there is no sin."[1]

ADAM'S FAMILY TREE: GENESIS 5

The details of the births and deaths of Adam's descendants through Seth in Genesis 5 enable us to construct a timeline from Creation to the Flood. Adam, the first man (1 Corinthians 15:45 & 47), and Eve, the mother of all living (Genesis 3:20), were created on Day Six of the Creation week in Year 1 A.H.[2] Seth was born 130 A.H., and so on through to Noah, who was 500 years old before his sons, Shem, Ham and Japheth, were born. Noah's father, Lamech, died in 1651 A.H., five years before his own father Methuselah. 1656 A.H. was the year of the Flood. Noah and his three sons connect the antediluvian and postdiluvian worlds of mankind.

THE GLOBAL FLOOD: GENESIS 6-9

After Adam's initial transgression, the next recorded sin is when Cain murdered his brother Abel (4:3-16), showing that the Devil, the evil one, continued to be active in the fallen world (compare 1 John 3:12). Although, when Enosh was born to Seth, "people began to call upon the name of the LORD" (4:26), the majority of mankind increased in wickedness. The wickedness of men became so bad, and the thoughts of their hearts were only evil continually, that God was grieved in His heart to such an extent that He decided to destroy all created things on the earth (6:5-7). Corruption reached crisis point in Noah's lifetime, when violence filled the earth (6:11).

So God destroyed the antediluvian world of mankind, along with the habitable earth and all that was in it by

38

means of a worldwide flood. Only Noah and his wife, his three sons and their wives (and all those animals and birds which God caused to go into the ark — 7:14-16), were preserved through the Flood by means of the ark. As Peter informs us in his second epistle,[3] that world order (the cosmos) – the whole earth with all its people and all animals and all birds on it – perished when it was completely flooded/deluged with water. The same word of God that had separated the land from the seas on Day Three of the creation week (1:9-10) now commanded the stored water, "the fountains of the great deep", to burst forth and the windows of the heavens to open (7:11). It rained forty days and forty nights (7:12). All the high mountains were submerged to a depth of about 6.75 metres (7:20). The flood waters prevailed on the earth for 150 days (7:24). It was a *total global catastrophe*. The topography of the whole earth was changed in this upheaval. So the world we see today is different from the earth as originally created. But there are present day proofs of the global flood, such as the worldwide existence of fossils.

THE TRUE HISTORY OF THE NATIONS: GENESIS 10

Genesis 10 is the fourth of the "generation" summaries in Genesis.[4] It differs from the others in that it is about generations of three people – Noah's sons. The intent is to provide a true history of every nation in the post-diluvian world, so that we know that all mankind descended from Adam *via* Noah. "The God who made the world and everything in it, being Lord of heaven and earth, … made from one man every nation of mankind to live on all the face of the earth, having determined allotted periods and the boundaries of their dwelling place, that they should seek God, in the hope that they might feel their way toward him and find him" (Acts

17:24-27). In Genesis 10, verse 32 is an important conclusion of the 'table of nations', "These are the clans of the sons of Noah, according to their genealogies, in their nations, and from these the nations spread abroad on the earth after the flood."

THE GLOBAL DISPERSION: GENESIS 11

Genesis 10:8-10 is another important section of history because it introduces Nimrod, a person with an ego to match his big reputation in the immediate postdiluvian world, "a mighty hunter before the LORD." He established his kingdom at Babel in the land of Shinar. Although God had told Noah and his sons to spread out and fill the whole earth (9:1 & 7), their descendants chose to settle down in the plain of Shinar (11:2). With the Flood as recent history, and Noah still alive upon the earth (he died 2006 A.H.), their evil intentions soon became clear. In direct opposition to the word of God, they joined together and said, "Come on, let us build ourselves a city and a tower, the top of which [may reach] to the heavens; and let us make ourselves a name, lest we be *scattered over the face of the whole earth*" (verse 4, N.Tr. with my emphasis). God recognized that this scheme was the beginning of people's determination to assert their combined will without any reference to Him, their Creator, and to raise themselves up as gods. This was a sin of the same magnitude as Adam's. God immediately intervened in judgment to disrupt the tower of Babel project. He said, "Come, let us go down and there confuse their language, so that they may not understand one another's speech" (verse 7). The building project was abandoned because God confused their languages (Babel meaning *confusion*). His judgment was intended to put a stop to this anti-God movement.

Again, it is vital to believe that this is the true history of the languages in the world, and that at this time God dispersed mankind from Babel over the face of all the earth, with the result that people came to live in every part of the world. This global dispersion probably took place during Peleg's lifetime, for 10:25 states, "for in his days the earth was divided" (Peleg meaning *division*). According to Genesis 10 Peleg was the fifth generation from Noah. He was born one hundred years after the Flood in 1757 A.H., and he died in 1996 A.H. It is staggering to realise that it only took a couple of hundred years or so for postdiluvian mankind to manifest the same kind of evils as their antediluvian forebears! Thankfully, Shem's "generations" (11:10-26) give hope. From Shem's "generations" arose Terah's "generations" (verses 27-32), which include Abram, who was born in 2008 A.H. – 2 years after the death of Noah.

THE CREATOR TO THE RESCUE

As soon as Adam and Eve sinned, they realised they were naked. They used fig leaves to make loincloths for themselves (3:7). They hid from God because these coverings were inadequate (3:8-10). But God provided garments of animal skins to clothe them properly (3:21). He also promised the defeat of Satan through Eve's seed (3:15). Then He prevented access to the tree of life (3:22-24). By these actions God gave the first indications of His plan of salvation. When man became so evil that God had to judge the world by the global Flood, He provided salvation for Noah and his family by means of the ark (6:8 – 8:19). After the Flood, God started anew by blessing Noah's family (9:1). He provided meat as food to sustain human life in the changed climatic conditions of postdiluvian world (9:2-7). He established an everlasting covenant with every living creature, signified by the rainbow (9:8-17), with the words, "I will never again curse the ground because of man, for the intention of man's heart is evil from his youth. Neither will I ever again strike down every living creature as I have done. While the earth remains, seedtime and harvest, cold and heat, summer and winter, day and night, shall not cease" (8:21-22).

But in the process of time Noah got drunk, and Ham's actions were an indication that men were going their own way again (9:18-29). As just shown, very soon after the Flood, they set about excluding God altogether at Babel. The global dispersion by which God judged them (see above) did not change their minds. Rather, as Romans 1:18-32 reveal, mankind only increased in ungodliness and unrighteousness. So God abandoned them to their own reprobate mind. From such a world (see Joshua 24:14), He called out Abram (Abraham), the father of the faithful (Genesis 12:1-3; Romans 4:16 & Galatians 3:7-9). Through Melchizedek, Abram was specifically blessed by "the Possessor (or, Creator, footnote) of heaven and earth" (Genesis 14:18-20 compare Hebrews 5:6 & chapter 7). And to Abraham the promise was made that from his Seed (Christ) salvation and blessing would come for all families/nations of the earth (Genesis 12:3 & 22:18; Galatians 3:8-9, 14 & 16).

Part 2
Biblical
teaching about
Creation

Chapter 4
New Testament teaching about Creation

WHAT PROMINENCE IS GIVEN TO THE TRUTH ABOUT CREATION IN THE NEW TESTAMENT?

"In over fifty years as a Christian I haven't heard much spoken ministry on biblical creation." So commented a friend of mine after reading my article "Is it necessary to believe in biblical creation?" in *Scripture Truth* magazine. But there is a *huge* amount of literature about creation! Most published expositions start with Genesis 1:1 and work forward through Scripture. Certainly "the everlasting gospel" (compare Revelation 14:6-7), that is, the witness that God is the Creator, continues throughout the whole of man's history. But there is further revelation concerning creation in the New Testament. Therefore, by starting our detailed analysis of the Bible's teaching about creation with the *New* Testament we see better its fundamental importance to the Christian faith:

- First and foremost, the New Testament revelation is what tells us that Christ Himself is the Creator, the Person by whom God created all things.

- As His disciples, we must give priority to the teaching of our Lord and Master. On all matters of Christian faith, of primary importance to us is the question, "What did *He* say?" In this case, about creation! And we must not succumb to the ever-present danger of ignoring His teaching, adapting it to fit in with current scientific teaching, or subjugating it to someone's interpretation of the Genesis account. "If anyone teaches a different doctrine and does not agree with the sound words of our Lord Jesus Christ and the teaching that accords with godliness, he is puffed up with conceit and understands nothing. ..." (1 Timothy 6:3-4).

CREATION IS CHRIST-CENTRED

New Testament teaching about creation focuses on the Person of Christ Himself. For example, the fact that He is the Creator is identified as one of His distinctive glories in the passages which highlight the unique excellences and glories of His Person:

- "In these last days [God] has spoken to us by his Son ... through whom also he created the world" (Hebrews 1:2).

- "All things were made through him; and without him was not anything made that was made" (John 1:3).

- "By him all things were created, in heaven and on earth, visible and invisible, whether thrones or dominions or rulers or authorities – all things were created through him and for him. And he is before all things, and in him all things hold together" (Colossians 1:16-17).

- Hebrews 1:3 and Colossians 1:17 both state that the creation relies upon Him not only for its beginning but also for its very continuance; and each by the word of His power!

- As its Creator, He will bring it to an end. "Lord, … the earth … and the heavens are the work of your hands; they will perish, but you remain; they will all wear out like a garment, like a robe you will roll them up, like a garment they will be changed. But you are the same, and your years will have no end" (Hebrews 1:10-12).

When we go back to read the account of creation in the Old Testament, we do so in the light of New Testament revelations such as these – that the Son carries out all the works of God on behalf of the Father (compare John 3:35 with 5:19-36).

CREATION IS CHRIST-CERTIFIED

During forty years as a quality professional, I've certified many a batch of drug substance as "made to the correct standard and of the right quality". I was professionally qualified to do so, even though I was not directly involved in its production. But the Lord Jesus, being the Agent of creation, can certify that God actually did create, and we implicitly believe His words. And His telling phrase in this regard is, *"the creation that God created"* (Mark 13:19, my emphasis).

The Lord's words on this matter extend to the importance and uniqueness of human beings in comparison to the rest of creation. When asked about divorce, He referred to God's provision of family life (marriage) at their creation for their wellbeing, "But from the beginning of creation, 'God made them male and female.' 'Therefore a man shall leave his father and mother and hold fast to his wife, and they shall become one flesh.' So they are no longer two but one flesh. What therefore

God has joined together, let not man separate" (Mark 10:6-9). Note here that the Lord directly connects "the beginning of creation" (i.e., Genesis 1:1) with "God made them male and female" (i.e., Genesis 1:27) – there is no time gap! More emphatically, He stated that mankind existed "from the foundation of the world" (Luke 11:50).

The Gospels display the Lord Jesus as the Creator-in-action. He changed water into wine; healed all kinds of sickness; opened deaf ears; gave sight to the blind; stilled the storm; walked on water; had command over demons; and raised the dead. In Luke 22:51 when Peter cut off Malchus' right ear, a simple touch from the Lord gave him a new one! There was no search in the dark for the amputated ear, no operation to stitch it back on, and no convalescent period of recovery, etc.

The majority of Christ's miracles were instantly accomplished by His commands, and this instantaneousness validates the creation account. The Psalmist captures this point when he exults, "For he spoke, and it came to be; he commanded, and it stood firm" (Psalm 33:9). In John 4:46-54, the official's son was healed by Jesus even speaking from some distance away!

The Lord's certification of creation was therefore both by words and by deeds.

CHRIST'S CLAIMS OF LORDSHIP OVER CREATION

The Sabbath was the seventh day of the creation week, when God rested from all His work (Genesis 1:31 – 2:2). In Mark 2:23-27, when challenged about His disciples' activities on the Sabbath, the Lord Jesus was able to explain the divine intent of the day of rest: "the Sabbath was made for man, not man for the Sabbath". In verse

28, He went on to claim total authority over it. As the Creator, He rightly insisted that He, the Son of Man, was also Lord of the Sabbath. The Lord Jesus demonstrated this authority by performing miracles on Sabbath days.[1] This authority could only mean that He was God (compare Mark 2:7-12). In John 5:17, He implied that He and His Father could not rest in a creation which had been spoiled by man's sin.

BELIEVERS' CONFIDENCE IN THE CREATOR

Hebrews 11:3 makes clear that believers know through faith *how* God created, "By faith we understand that the universe was created by the word of God, so that what is seen was not made out of things that are visible." Romans 1:20 insists that mankind has clearly understood God's creative power ever since the beginning of time. But by faith believers discern *how* God created, that it was by His all-powerful word. He created the universe from nothing, *ex nihilo*, from no pre-existing materials. As Romans 4:17 teaches, "God ... calls into existence the things that do not exist." In Hebrews 11:3:

- "The word "created" is usually translated "framed", and denotes the process of the fulfilment of the divine will.[2]
- "The word of God" is *rhema* and alludes to the phrase "the Lord said" in Genesis 1.[2]

By faith, believers know *who* created the universe. It was God in the Person of the Son (Hebrews 1:2). But they also know *why* there is a creation and for *what* purpose. These are questions which science can never answer. But the answers are found in Revelation 4:11, "Worthy are you, our Lord and God, to receive glory and honour and power, for you created all things, and by your will [pleasure, KJV] they existed and were created." Finally, believers have confidence that the Creator will sustain/uphold His creation by that same word of His power by which He spoke it into existence – until He decides to dispose of it (Hebrews 1:3 & 12).

THE HOLY SPIRIT'S COMMENTARY ON CREATION

Augustine of Hippo said that the Old Testament is made clear by ("lies open in") the New Testament. The Holy Spirit's commentary in the New Testament on creation and subsequent happenings in the Genesis account is very informative. For example, 2 Peter 3:5-7, "there were heavens from of old, and an earth compacted out of the water and amidst water, by the word of God; by *which* means the world that then was, being overflowed with water, perished; but the heavens that now are, and the earth, by *the same word* have been stored up for fire, being reserved against the day of judgment and destruction of ungodly men" (ASV, my emphases).

We know that God created *by His word*.[3] Peter here tells us that the judgment of the Flood[4] was executed *by His word* and that this present creation is reserved for judgment *by His word*. There is a remarkable statement here! There was an earth before the flood, which was quite different from the present earth, because the antediluvian world order (the cosmos) perished in the global catastrophe. Yes, the Creator is active throughout history, dictating the course of world events. He will intervene again with the catastrophic events of "the Day of the Lord"[5] (verse 10), when the earth will be reshaped[6] for the Millennium. Earth's final catastrophe will be one of total destruction by fire (verses 10-12), followed by the creation of the new heavens and a new earth (verse 13), so that men can enjoy the coming "day of God" (verse 12).

THE IMPORTANCE OF CREATION TO NEW TESTAMENT DOCTRINES

You cannot read the New Testament without finding what happened at creation to be the underpinning of its teachings at every turn!

THE IMPORTANCE OF CREATION TO THE GOSPEL

In his exposition of the Gospel in Romans, Paul teaches that sin and death were brought into the world by Adam's transgression (Romans 5:12-21). These verses contrast the two heads – Adam the head of the sinful race of mankind; and Christ the Head of the new race of believers. Notice what Paul means in verse 12. He means that there was no death in the world before the Fall! Adam's sin had a consequential effect upon everything that he had been given dominion over.[7] Under Adam, everything ends in death. By contrast, Jesus Christ was obedient even unto death so that "in Christ Jesus" the outcome is eternal life (verse 21). If we deny the historicity of Adam, we destroy the basis for believing in the fundamental effects of the death of Christ for humanity.

THE IMPORTANCE OF CREATION WITH RESPECT TO SUFFERING

In Romans 8:19-23, Paul explains that Man's fall also brought down the whole sphere of his dominion[7] (verse 21). Paul goes on to explain that the Gospel gives an answer to these tragedies of life. They will be reversed for the whole of the restored creation[8] when believers reign with Christ. Yes, the Gospel shows God to be "a faithful Creator". Peter contains much teaching about the ways in which, and why, Christians suffer. He advises all such to trust themselves to the faithful Creator's care (1 Peter 4:19), that is, the Person who subjected the creation in hope of its coming release (Romans 8:20-21).

THE IMPORTANCE OF CREATION TO RESURRECTION

In his great resurrection thesis in 1 Corinthians 15, Paul again contrasts Adam and Christ. He identifies the Lord Jesus Christ as the last Adam and the second Man (verses 45-48), who gives us the victory over death. In a comprehensive sweep of the unstoppable course of Christ's resurrection in verses 20-28, Paul again refers back to creation and the situation pre/post the Fall. Here, Paul teaches another essential doctrine of the Gospel. It is that resurrection must come through man because death came through the first man, Adam, and in him all men die. Verses 35-54 expands the teaching further by explaining in detail how, in resurrection, believers will bear the image of the heavenly One. Fundamental to this teaching is that all men come from Adam, the first man who was created by God out of the dust of the earth.

THE IMPORTANCE OF CREATION TO ASPECTS OF GODLINESS

In 1 Timothy 4:3-6, Paul advises Timothy that teachers should be trained in "the words of the faith and of the good doctrine" that have their foundation in a good and caring Creator who provided every creature as food for man (compare Genesis 9:3). God's providential care for His creatures is also emphasised by the Lord Jesus in Matthew 6:25-34 & Luke 12:22-34, where He teaches His disciples to rely upon God to provide food and clothing. The godly person is content with these provisions (1 Timothy 6:8).

THE IMPORTANCE OF CREATION TO MARRIAGE

As I have already commented on above, the Lord Jesus Christ referred His hearers back to the creation account when they questioned about marriage (Mark 10:2-12). He answered, "From the beginning of creation, 'God made them male and female'" (verse 6). Marriage was God's idea for the benefit of mankind's life upon earth; and He alone defines what it is (verse 7). It is a man joined in union to a woman, his wife, to become one flesh for the entirety of life together (verses 8-9). The Lord said it cannot be altered to mean something else, nor interfered with at all by any person or governments of men (verse 9). Any other union, or definition, is a fake!

THE IMPORTANCE OF CREATION TO HEADSHIP

The teaching of headship in 1 Corinthians 11:2-16 flows out from the doctrine of marriage given by God at creation (Genesis 2:18-25). The order of creation is clearly taught in 1 Corinthians 11:3:

- God, the Originator of creation (compare 1 Corinthians 8:6), is head over Christ, that is, His anointed Man, who is the Agent of creation.

- Christ is head over man, who is the pinnacle of God's creation.

- The man is head over the woman because she was made from man. This is based directly upon God's creatorial ordering of mankind. Paul provides the proof of this from the Genesis account of creation by stating that Adam was created first, and then Eve was formed from Adam (verses 8-9).

God intends that headship be practically demonstrated when men and women pray to Him and/or prophesy, that is, speak on His behalf (verses 4-16). Paul also insists on man's authority in headship (and woman's subjection) in 1 Timothy 2, by again emphasising that Adam was formed before Eve. He adds an explanatory comment that Eve was deceived into usurping Adam's authority at the Fall (verses 13-14). His intention in writing these instructions to Timothy is so that he "may know how one ought to behave in the household of God, which is the church of the living God, a pillar and buttress of truth" (3:15).

THE IMPORTANCE OF CREATION AS TO NEW CREATION

In 2 Corinthians 4:4-6, Paul contrasts the work of God in new creation with the original physical creation, when he talks about believers responding to the message of the Gospel, "For God, who said, 'Let light shine out of darkness,' has shone in our hearts to give the light of the knowledge of the glory of God in the face of Jesus Christ" (verse 6). The actions of God in Genesis 1 picture for us His work in new creation in us. And the new creation of all things is in and through His Son.[9]

CONCLUSION: CREATION IS FOR CHRIST

"There is one God, the Father, from whom are all things and for whom we exist, and one Lord, Jesus Christ, through whom are all things and through whom we exist" (1 Corinthians 8:6).

Creation finds its source in the Father and its ultimate fulfilment in His eternal purpose. These purposes concern His Son, our Lord Jesus Christ, who brought all creation into being, and through whom there is new creation. Therefore, the importance of creation, and man's place in that creation, cannot be overestimated. It has to do with the glory and honour which the Father deems to be due to the Son (compare John 5:23). It is all for Him, the "heir of all things" (Hebrews 1:2). And we, God's children, are to share that glory with Him (Romans 8:17)! Eliminate biblical creation, and you fatally weaken New Testament teaching regarding the person of Christ, His Gospel and its effects; and many other matters!

Chapter 5
Old Testament teaching about Creation

THE FULLNESS OF TESTIMONY TO GOD AS CREATOR THROUGHOUT THE OLD TESTAMENT

Old Testament writers constantly hark back to the Creation and in doing so reveal interesting additional information about God and how He created. What they write enhances our appreciation of the Creator. God Himself confronted Job with these very things. In Job 38-41 three main attributes of God, as demonstrated in creation, stand out:

- By His perfect wisdom God knew *what* to create to bring glory to Himself and blessing to the master-piece of His creation – man.

- By His perfect understanding God knew *how* to create everything.

- By His perfect power as the Almighty God He had the intrinsic *capability* to create what He had planned.

By God's wisdom

"The LORD by wisdom founded the earth; by understanding He established the heavens" (Proverbs 3:19).

My wife often says that one of the blessings of ministering the Gospel to very young children is that they already know within their hearts that God exists. Despite this, many adults are in denial of this truth (compare Romans 1:20-22). In Ecclesiastes 3:11, Solomon declares, "[God] has made everything beautiful in its time. Also, he has put eternity into man's heart, yet so that he cannot find out what God has done from the beginning to the end." The very best that present-day non-Christian intellectuals will admit is that He is the Intelligent Designer. But God is more than that! Sagacious Solomon, with his God-given understanding of the natural world (compare 1 Kings 4:29-34) declares in the proverb given above that God used His infinite wisdom (knowing *what* was required) and understanding (knowing *how* to do it) to design and to make the universe. David also appreciated this when he viewed its vastness (Psalm 8:1 & 3); and again when he pondered the complexities of his own being (Psalm 139:13-18). With modern technological advances, we now know much more about the hugeness of the cosmos, as well as about the intricacies of the smallest of created things, such as the 'simple cell'[1] of a living organism. These complexities of the creation, and of life itself, only reinforce in us (believers) what David felt about these things, and convince us of the supreme wisdom of our Creator.

In Proverbs 8:22-31, Wisdom is personified and calls Himself the "master craftsman" (verse 30, NKJV). This is an apposite description for the Creator, because in all the works of God, the Son does exactly what the Father shows Him (compare John 5:19-20). But Colossians 1:16 specifically attributes creation to the Son, "For by [or, in] Him all things were created," where the word "in" implies the wisdom, as well as the power, to create (N.Tr. footnote).

BY GOD'S POWER AND WISDOM

"But the LORD is the true God; he is the living God and the everlasting King. ... It is he who made the earth by his power, who established the world by his wisdom, and by his understanding stretched out the heavens" (Jeremiah 10:10 & 12; similarly 51:15).

These verses assert that the power of God (i.e., His ability to create) is commensurate with His wisdom. Paul clearly states this in Romans 1:20, "For his invisible attributes, namely, his eternal power and divine nature, have been clearly perceived, ever since the creation of the world, in the things that have been made. So [the whole of mankind is] without excuse." Christians know that Christ is both the *power* and the *wisdom* of God (1 Corinthians 1:24). J. G. Deck's hymn to the "Lamb of God" aptly states,

> Thy almighty power and wisdom
> all creation's works proclaim:
> heaven and earth alike confess Thee
> as the ever great I AM. [2]

SCRIPTURAL ANTHROPOMORPHISM

"Anthropomorphism" is a figure of speech much used throughout Scripture. This is the practice of attributing human action (or form) to God, and it is often used to aid our understanding of God's creative activities. For example, in Genesis 2:7, "the LORD God formed the man of dust from the ground and breathed into his nostrils the breath of life, and the man became a living creature." This explains how God made Adam and, in an intimate way, made him unique amongst all creatures (compare 1:27). Isaiah 29:16 & 64:8 even describe God as the Potter and man the clay that He moulds and uses to accomplish His sovereign will (compare Romans 9:19-24). He declares in Isaiah 43:7, "everyone ... whom I created for my glory, whom I formed and made."

However, in reality God is spirit – He is without physical form or shape. We know from the repetitive phrase, "And God said,"[3] that God simply spoke the whole creation into being; but we have already seen the other "anthropomorphism" of God making the universe as a craftsman makes an object. Hence other Scriptures develop this picture and elaborate on how God "laid the foundation(s) of the earth", "established the earth/ heavens/world"[4], and "stretched out the heavens"[5]; and they speak about the work of His outstretched arm, of His hands, of His fingers, and so on.

LAYING THE FOUNDATION AND ESTABLISHING THE EARTH

"Of old you laid the foundation of the earth ..." (Psalm 102:25).

"Your faithfulness endures to all generations; you have established the earth, and it stands fast" (Psalm 119:90).

Like any builder, God started with the foundation of the earth[6] on Day One of creation (Genesis 1:1-5) and then built up from this core during the creation week. (In the New Testament, the expressions "from/since the foundation of the world"[7] and "before the foundation of the world"[8] are used to indicate the very earliest points in time.) Having laid the foundation in the beginning (that is, on Day One), God built up the earth on Day Three. He established (prepared, made ready, perfected)[9] it for habitation by the animals, but more especially, by mankind (Isaiah 45:18). He did this by "spread[ing] out the earth above the waters" (Psalm 136:6). He also filled the earth with plants and vegetation, "spread[ing] out the earth and what comes from it ..." (Isaiah 42:5), which He did entirely by Himself (Isaiah 44:24).

GOD'S OUTSTRETCHED ARM, HIS HANDS AND HIS FINGERS

"Ah, LORD God! It is you who have made the heavens and the earth by your great power and by your outstretched arm! Nothing is too hard for you" (Jeremiah 32:17).

"It was my hands that stretched out the heavens, and I commanded all their host" (Isaiah 45:12).

"Your heavens [are] the work of your fingers, the moon and the stars, which you have set in place" (Psalm 8:3).

God's "outstretched arm" is a frequently-used Old Testament anthropomorphism to describe how God employed His almighty creatorial power – as in the first quotation (and in Jeremiah 27:5) – but also at work in His redemption, protection, and judgement of Israel.[10] The recurrent expression, He "stretched out the heavens"[5] explains how He took the heavens He had made on Day One (Genesis 1:1) and established them for mankind (Proverbs 3:19 & 8:27). On Day Four, the day when He "made the stars also" (Genesis 1:16, KJV), God stretched out the universe as we would do with a tent or curtains (Psalm 104:2 & Isaiah 40:22). We noted previously that God used His own understanding and almighty power (Jeremiah 51:15) to give us our universe, whose vast distances scientists measure in terms of light years.[12] He is the Almighty who acted alone and unaided, "by myself" (Isaiah 44:24). In Isaiah 48:13 God says this was the work of His *right hand* and thus emphasises His power.

Genesis 1:17 states that on Day Four of creation God set the solar system (the sun, the moon and the planets) and the galaxies in position to give light to the earth. God carefully and accurately placed them in outer space as a skilled constructor would use his fingers for the more intricate positioning of his model. The result is that the sun is in exactly the correct position to sustain life on earth.[11] When David says in Psalm 8:3 that the stars were also the work of God's fingers, he indicates that the stretching out of the heavens was a controlled event, not an explosion, not a "Big Bang"! God's control over the entire universe is such that, "He stretches out the north over the void and hangs the earth on nothing" (Job 26:7).

THE STARS

"He determines the number of the stars; he gives to all of them their names. Great is our Lord, and abundant in power; his understanding is beyond measure" (Psalm 147:4-5).

Stuart Burgess gives the scientific estimate of the number of stars in the universe as least 50 billion billion.[13] The actual number is indeterminable by man (Genesis 15:5). But at creation, God both assigned the actual number of stars and individually named each one of them! "He who brings out their host by number, calling them all by name, by the greatness of His might, and because He is strong in power not one is missing" (Isaiah 40:26). These names are not revealed to us. In Scripture God uses names that mankind recognises, such as Pleiades, Orion, the Mazzaroth and the Great Bear (Job 38:31-32). Each star has a specific purpose in creation, "for star differs from star in glory" (1 Corinthians 15:41).

THE BEAUTY OF THE UNIVERSE

"By his Spirit the heavens are adorned ..." (Job 26:13, N.Tr.).

God has given the universe grandeur and exquisite beauty, the glory of which bears constant witness to Him (Psalm 19:1-4). This 'Song of Creation' has been, and will continue to be, proclaimed to the whole of mankind (and in this clear, understandable way!) throughout all the ages of the history of the world. "The heavens declare the glory of God, and the sky above proclaims his handiwork" (verse 1). Amen! Many Old Testament writers exude appreciation of the glory of God's creation seen both on earth and in heaven. It is appropriate to finish this chapter with praise from one of them, David the Psalmist, "O LORD, our Lord, how majestic is your name in all the earth! You have set your glory above the heavens" (Psalm 8:1).

REMEMBERING MY CREATOR SINCE MY YOUTH

Part 3
Creation in the
Old Testament

Chapter 6
Creation Mega-Themes throughout Old Testament History

Chapter 5 focussed on frequently recurring metaphors of God's creatorial activity. This Chapter looks at what it meant to Old Testament people to know and be in relationship with the God who created the universe – from three writers, Job, Isaiah, and Jeremiah, each of whom refer to the greatness of God in creation. Job's knowledge of God as Creator led him to repent and worship. God revealed to Isaiah and Jeremiah that the disasters that befell their nation were in the hand of the God of creation, whose power was the guarantee of new covenant blessing.

FROM JOB

Job probably lived about the time of Abraham.[1] In those times the saints knew God as El Shaddai (God Almighty), the great Creator and Protector (compare Genesis 17:1). This Name of God occurs more often in Job than any other Old Testament book (5:17, 6:4, etc.). Job records how godly non-Hebrews (1:1) viewed God and His creation. In fact the witness they had to God was mainly the witness of creation to "his eternal power and Godhead" (Romans 1:20, KJV). Job and his friends glorified God as God; unlike the rest of mankind who had given up God (a similar worldview is prevalent today!). As mentioned in the previous Chapter (Chapter 5), the LORD's own words in Job 38-41 are a self-revelation of His three main attributes – His perfect wisdom, His perfect understanding, and His perfect power. Job acknowledges God's activity in His creation, as One doing great, unsearchable and marvellous things (5:9) such as controlling the rainfall (5:10) and commanding the sun and the stars (9:7). Elihu describes some of His wondrous works in nature in chapter 37 – thunder and lightning, snow and ice, gentle and torrential rains, hurricanes, cold and hot winds, etc. And God alone could tame great creatures extant in those days – Behemoth (40:15-24), Leviathan (chapter 41) and Rahab (9:13 & 26:12).[2] Most significantly, Job recognised God had fashioned and made him (10:8-11 & 31:15). In addition to these great points, the book of Job also reveals the healthy fear of God that arises from the knowledge of Him as the Creator – for example, chapter 9, where verses 14-34 follow on from verses 4-12. The crux of Job's problem was whether even a just man, such as he, had any "rights" before his Creator God? The answer to that question, which, as we now know, is fully explained in the Gospel, Job discovered when God spoke directly to him (compare 40:1-5 with 42:1-6).

FROM ISAIAH

BACKGROUND HISTORY

Isaiah wrote in times of national declension in Israel, when the northern king of Assyria (with the kingdom of

Babylon a distant rumble on the horizon) began reasserting itself in the world. Chapters 1-39 deal with the fact that the immediate threat from Ephraim and Syria would be replaced by that of the Assyrian invasion; and the promise of deliverances for Zion. In 721 B.C., the northern kingdom of Israel was deported by Shalmaneser, the king of Assyria (2 Kings 17:1-23 with 18:9-12). Not very many years later, Sennacherib, the next-but-one king of Assyria, took all the fortified cities of Judah, as prophesied in Isaiah 8:5-8 & chapters 28-31. At this point in their history Hezekiah was told by Isaiah to rely solely upon God for deliverance (chapters 36-37), which came miraculously in one night (37:36-37). After describing this deliverance, and to allay Judah's fear both of Assyria and of future world superpowers, Isaiah reminded the people of Judah in chapter 40 of Someone far greater, who they had been told about from the beginning of time, that is, from the foundations of the earth (40:21).

COMFORT MY PEOPLE, CHAPTER 40

The little kingdom of Judah was puny indeed relative to the superpowers; but the people were to remember the character of the Creator in all His wisdom, greatness, power, and ability (40:13-14, 22, 25-26 & 28). Perhaps the most comforting message for them in this pivotal chapter was verse 17, "All the nations are as nothing before Him, they are accounted by Him as less than nothing and emptiness." Why? Because the Lord GOD is so great that He was able at creation to measure out the waters in the hollow of His hand and to mark off the heavens with the span of His hand. He enclosed the dust of the earth in a measure and weighed the mountains in a balance and the hills in scales! (verse 12). To Him, all nations are a mere drop from a bucket and totally insignificant – like the fine dust on the scales [or balances, KJV][3] – and the isles like an atom! (verse 15, N.Tr.). By God's methods of computing, they are "less than nothing and emptiness" (verse 17). He is so far above and beyond them that they appear as grasshoppers to Him (verse 22). So, whether it be the mighty Assyrian or the mightier Babylonian king or any of his successors, "[He reduces] princes to nothing, and makes the rulers of the earth as emptiness" (verse 23). No sooner would they rise, than they would disappear (verse 24); and that at His command (41:2-4). And this was the God who would never forget Jacob (40:27-28).

I AM HE

For Israel's Saviour is the enduring, everlasting God, who is ready, willing, and able to help everyone who relies on Him (40:28-31). Addressing the nations directly, God asks, in verse 41:4a, "Who has performed and done this [with these world powers], calling the generations from the beginning?" Assertively, He provides His own answer in verse 4b, "I, the LORD, the first, and with the last; I am He." "I am He" can be translated, "'I, THE SAME,' ... it is really a name of God" (N.Tr. footnote, verse 4). In Isaiah it is a dominant Name of the unchanging Creator God (e.g., 43:10, 13 & 25).[4] He is called "the God of the whole earth" (54:5) with sovereign rights because He created both heaven and earth (e.g., 37:16).[5]

CYRUS

These sovereign rights are especially emphasized in the Salvation Oracle concerning Cyrus (44:24 – 45:13), written some two hundred years before the heathen Persian monarch existed! "I am the LORD, who made all things, who alone stretched out the heavens, who spread out the earth by myself...who says of Cyrus, 'He is my shepherd and he shall fulfill my purpose'" (44:24 & 28, compare Ezra 1:1-4). Remarkably, God speaks directly to Cyrus, even though Cyrus does not personally know the LORD, and appoints him to office so that all peoples of the world should know that there is no other God besides the LORD (45:1-7). Isaiah 45 verses 9 & 11-13 provide a stern warning to anyone who would resist God's sovereign will with respect to Cyrus's destiny. "Woe to him who strives with his [i.e., Cyrus's] Maker! Let the potsherd strive with the potsherds of the earth! Shall the clay say to him who forms it, 'What are you making?' Or shall your handiwork say, 'He has no hands'? ... Thus says the LORD, the Holy One of Israel, and his Maker, '... I have made the earth, and created man on it. I – My hands – stretched out the heavens, and all their host I have commanded. I have raised him [Cyrus] up in righteousness, and I will direct all his ways; he shall build My city [Jerusalem] and let My exiles [of Israel] go free, not for price nor reward,' says the LORD of hosts" (45:9-13, NKJV).

ISRAEL, GOD'S SPECIAL CREATION

Salvation for Israel, then and in the future, is because the nation was created to belong to the LORD. "Thus says the LORD, he who created[6] you, O Jacob, he who formed[7] you, O Israel, 'Fear not, for I have redeemed you; I have called you by name, you are mine'" (43:1). Israel is the Creator's "treasured possession among all peoples, for all the earth is [his]" (Exodus 19:5). Moreover, when the comforting message of Isaiah 43:1 is resumed in verse 7, it is each individual of saved Israel[8] who is created, redeemed and called by Jehovah. "Everyone [of Israel] who is called by my name, whom I created[6] for my glory, whom I formed[7] and made.[9] ... I am the LORD, your Holy One, the Creator of Israel, your King" (verse 7 with verse 15 – see also 44:21 & 24). The three statements at the end of verse 7 use each of the words employed throughout the Old Testament to describe God's creative actions: created,[6] formed[7] and made.[9] W. E. Vine comments, "[These] three statements ... form a progress to a climax:

1 "I have created him for My glory"; that expresses the thought of His power in bringing the nation into being;

2 "I have formed him"; that points to the process of His transforming grace by which the one created is made to reflect His glory;

3 "Yea, I have made him"; this points to the completion of the divine act. The verb rendered "I have made" signifies more than simply to make, it conveys the thought of bringing a work to perfection."[10]

These comments could also be made about *creation itself*, as well as Israel.

The future promised to the nation of Israel is a significant part of God's sovereign plan for the future of the whole creation, especially the earth. "But Israel is saved by the LORD with everlasting salvation; you shall not be put to shame or confounded to all eternity. For thus says the LORD, who created[6] the heavens (He is God!), who formed[7] the earth and made[9] it (He established it; He did not create[6] it empty, He formed[7] it to be inhabited!), 'I am the LORD, and there is no other. ... I the LORD speak the truth; I declare what is right'" (45:17-19). Therefore, Israel's calling is as sure as the created order of the universe (48:12-13 & 15). Her comfort and protection are directly from her Maker, who also made the heavens and the earth (51:12-13 & 15-16). She is in special relationship to her Maker – He is her Husband (54:5-10).

THE DAY OF THE LORD

Israel's final and complete salvation is dependent upon the Creator intervening and changing His creation to create new heavens and a new earth (65:17-18; 66:22). The blessed climax for Israel and the whole world will be when the Creator fully executes these judgments prophesied by Isaiah. He shall, in the Day of the LORD, "shake the earth mightily" by His majesty and power (2:19, NKJV). Whilst there is always symbolic meaning to such an expression, Isaiah makes many references to the Creator changing the established order of creation, especially the natural world, both in judgment and in subsequent millennial blessings.[11] For example:

- 11:6-9 describe a restored creation[12] with Edenic conditions. Isaiah 11 is literally true – there will be geographical/topographical changes to dry up the tongue of the Sea of Egypt and the River Euphrates and thus facilitate the recall of Israel and Judah (verses 12 & 15-16).

- In the oracle of Babylon's judgment, God announces that He will prevent the stars, sun and moon from giving light (13:10). "Therefore I will shake the heavens, and the earth will move out of her place, in the wrath of the LORD of hosts, and in the day of His fierce anger" (13:13, NKJV).

- The judgment will be so severe that, "Behold, the LORD will empty the earth and make it desolate, and He will twist its surface and scatter its inhabitants. … The foundations of the earth tremble. The earth is utterly broken, the earth is split apart, the earth is violently shaken" (24:1 & 18-19).

73

God's creatorial power will therefore be in action to make the earth ready for Messiah's kingdom in Israel. "Then the moon shall be confounded, and the sun ashamed; for the LORD of hosts shall reign in mount Zion, and in Jerusalem, and before his ancients gloriously" (24:23, RV).

FROM JEREMIAH

Jeremiah lived and prophesised during the very last days of the southern kingdom of Judah prior to its captivity (Jeremiah 1:1-3). He makes relatively few, but extremely significant, references to the person and action of the Creator. In those times people in the nations regarded military success as coming from their gods. But Jeremiah is able to proclaim to apostate Judah that the true God ever continues to be the living God; and that "the Portion of Jacob" formed all things (10:10-16, especially verse 12). Jeremiah repeats this message in 51:15-19 as part of the prophecy uttered against haughty Babylon (chapters 50-51) and just before he records (in chapter 52) the actual fall of Jerusalem at the hands of Nebuchadnezzar in 588 B.C. Perhaps Jeremiah is better known for his two famous prophecies, firstly, concerning the seventy-year' captivity of Judah (25:1-14 & chapter 29); and secondly, concerning the new covenant for both Israel and Judah (chapters 30-32). In relation to the captivity, the LORD told Jeremiah to tell the envoys who had come from the surrounding nations to king Zedekiah (presumably about the possibility of forming a united front against Nebuchadnezzar), "Thus says the LORD of hosts, the God of Israel, 'This is what you shall say to your masters: "It is I who by My great power and My outstretched arm have made the earth, with the men and animals that are on the earth, and I give it to whomever it seems right to Me. Now I have given all these lands into the hand of Nebuchadnezzar, the king of Babylon, my servant, and I have given him also the beasts of the field to serve him. All the nations shall serve him and his son and his grandson, until the time of his own land comes. Then many nations and great kings shall make him their slave"'" (27:4-7). In other words, through Jeremiah, God proclaimed to the nations that the Babylonian conquest was only an expression of His sovereign creatorial will (compare 51:12-15). But concerning His new covenant to Israel (31.31-34), God makes the vastness and fixed order of creation the surety of His promises (31:35-37 with 33:25-26).

Part 4
Creation in
the Psalms

Overview

CREATION IN PSALMS

Psalms are the songs of Israel, by which they worshipped and glorified God, and appealed to Him in their distress, both individual and national. This worship and glorification of God was founded upon who God is, as He had revealed Himself to them. Therefore they often celebrate the fact that He is the only God and the sole Creator of all things. They express a constant awareness that "All the gods of the peoples are worthless idols, but the LORD made the heavens" (Psalm 96:5). Israel's safety depended on the reliability of the promises made to them by this Creator God. Therefore the godly Israelite could "lift up [his] eyes to the hills", asking rhetorically (he is not 'asking' because he does not know, but to emphasise his conviction before the hearer/reader) where his help would come from (Psalm 121:1). The answer was, not from the hills themselves or anything *inside* creation, but "from the LORD who made heaven and earth" (verse 2). This sentiment is repeated (nationally) in Psalm 124:8, "Our help is in the name of the LORD, who made heaven and earth." And the greatest benediction they

79

could confer on each other was, in the words of Psalm 115:15, "May you be blessed by the LORD, who made the heaven and earth!" (Compare Psalm 134:3.)

Similarly Israel's national hopes for deliverance rested on their covenant God, who could control nature, who had performed miracles in Egypt, divided the sea in rescuing them from Egypt, and miraculously produced water from the flinty rock to sustain them in the desert (e.g., Psalm 77:11-19 & Psalm 114).[1] And yet, amazing as creation is, and as clear as is its witness to the compassion of the Saviour-God (e.g., Psalm 65:5-13 & Psalm 145:15-19), it does so incompletely, due to sin. Therefore some Psalms also celebrate the creatorial power that will introduce the glorious rule of Messiah, when there will be abundance of corn even on the tops of the mountains (Psalm 72:3 & 16).[2]

Chapter 7
Creation in Psalms Book 1

PSALM 8: ESTABLISHING THE CREATOR'S PRAISE

Psalms 1-8 can be viewed as introductory to the entire Psalter. As concluding this 'introduction', Psalm 8 provides the basis for all the creation themes found in all five books of Psalms. Primarily it celebrates both the glory of creation and man's (Adam's!) position in it. Its theme is *global praise*, as is shown by the fact that the opening and closing phrases of the Psalm (in verses 1a & 9, N.Tr.) are identical, "Jehovah our Lord, how excellent is thy name in all the earth!"

Tom Summerhill identifies three spheres wherein the Name of God is exalted – the earth, the starry heavens and the heaven of heavens (verses 1, 3 & 5).[1] But verse 1 finishes with "who hast set thy majesty above the heavens" (verse 1b, N.Tr.). "Majesty" suggests the visible manifestation of the Presence of Jehovah (1 Chronicles 29:11, Psalms 45:3 & 93:1), a majesty which, as we now know from 2 Peter 1:16-19, will be displayed in the physical kingdom of our Lord Jesus Christ. So, viewed prophetically, Psalm 8 anticipates the climax of this present creation – the universal reign of Christ as the

Son of Man. Where Adam failed in administration and stewardship, Christ will succeed when *He* is set over all the works of God's hand, not only in this terrestrial creation where Adam failed, but also over the astronomical and heavenly creation (compare Ephesians 1:10 & 22).[2] However, as Tom Summerhill asserts, "Meanwhile, God's glory remains unchallenged in paradise and in the astronomical universe."[1] Meanwhile, too, verse 3 reminds *us* to take account of the order God has established throughout His creation so that praise issues from our lips; for praise of the Creator is appropriate from saints of every dispensation! This leads us to Psalm 19.

PSALM 19: THE INCESSANT CREATION HYMN

Look up into the skies, especially at night, and what do you see? Verse 1 says that you will see undeniable evidence of the work of the Creator's hands in the beauty and splendour of the heavens, "The heavens declare the glory of God, and the sky above proclaims His handiwork." No one can ever deny their unfailing witness, for "Day to day pours out speech, and night to night reveals knowledge" (verse 2). That is true even though "There is no speech, and there are no words, yet their voice is heard" (verse 3, N.Tr.). The message is universal – there never has been, nor ever will be, a single member of the human race who is not confronted with the everlasting gospel of creation. "Their measuring line[3] goes out through all the earth, and their words to the end of the world" (verse 4a). Yet mankind continues in obstinate denial of the Creator (compare Romans 1:19-23)!

In verses 4b-6 the sun is suddenly brought into focus. "In them He has set a tent for the sun, which comes out like a bridegroom leaving his chamber, and, like a strong man, runs its course with joy. Its rising is from the end of the heavens, and its circuit to the end of them, and there is nothing hidden from its heat." If the vastness of the galaxies seen in the night skies points to the power and greatness of the Creator, the poetic language of verses 4b-6 witnesses to His nature and character. In His goodness He sustains every part of His world through the existence of the sun. He is its Source and the world's great, impartial Blesser (compare verse 6b with Matthew 5:45b)!

One day, the rejoicing of the heavens and the earth will bear testimony that the LORD is coming to judge the earth, that is, those peoples who have not responded to the testimony of creation (Psalm 96:11-13). But that dreadful Day has not yet come. Meanwhile, God has left another, fuller, witness to Himself alongside creation – His written word. Appropriately, then, verses 7-13 of Psalm 19 extol this other testimony.

PSALM 24: CREATION – IT'S ALL HIS!

The thought of the coming Day when God will reclaim His terrestrial world leads us to the theme of Psalm 24. The LORD is the King of glory who will claim the Kingdom because He has moral, official and personal rights to it – but, most fundamentally, because He has creatorial rights to it. "The earth is the LORD's and the fulness thereof [footnote, "all that fills it"], the world and those who dwell therein, for He has founded it upon the seas and established it upon the rivers" (verses 1-2). Creation belongs to Him, the Sovereign One ("the LORD's" in verse 1 and "he" in verse 2 are emphatic words in the Hebrew). The earth with all its fulness and populations were designed to give satisfaction and bring glory to their Creator. This will actually be so during the

Millennium, when "the earth will be filled with the knowledge of the glory of the LORD as the waters cover the sea" (Habakkuk 2:14 & Isaiah 11:9b).

God's ownership of creation is mentioned or implied in other Psalms, for example:

- "Ask of me, and I will make the nations your heritage, and the ends of the earth your possession ..." (Psalm 2:8).
- "For every beast of the forest is mine, the cattle on a thousand hills. I know all the birds of the hills, and all that moves in the field is mine" (Psalm 50:10-11).
- "Gilead is mine; Manasseh is mine; Ephraim is my helmet; Judah is my sceptre. Moab is my washbasin ..." (Psalm 60:7-8 & Psalm 108:8-9).
- "The heavens are yours; the earth also is yours; the world and all that is in it, you have founded them. The north and the south, you have created them; Tabor and Hermon joyously praise your name" (Psalm 89:11-12).
- "Know that the LORD, he is God! It is he who made us, and we are his (or, "not we ourselves," footnote); we are his people, and the sheep of his pasture" (Psalm 100:3).

This ownership by the Creator is emphasised in repeated descriptions of the LORD as the Maker of heaven, earth and sea (e.g., Psalm 95:5).[4] Yes, "he is our God" and we must listen to His voice (Psalm 95:7). This leads us to Psalm 29.

PSALM 29: GOD'S VOICE AND CREATION

Verses 3-9 describe the various physical effects that His voice has on His creation as the reason for all, including the heavenly beings [or, "sons of the mighty one", verse 1 (RV)], to ascribe glory to Him and to worship Him (verses 1-2). Verse 3 interprets His voice as thunder, "the God of glory thunders". David is emphasising that thunder is evidence of *the Creator's power*, not merely that of nature (compare "And God said" in the Genesis 1 creation account). This is suggested by the recurrence of it being "over the waters" in verse 3. The Creator's voice is heard seven times over in verses 3-9.

> O Lord my God! When I in awesome wonder
> Consider all the works Thy hand hath made,
> I see the stars, I hear the mighty thunder,
> Thy power throughout the universe displayed:
>
> Then sings my soul, my Saviour God to Thee,
> How great Thou art! How great Thou art!
> Then sings my soul, my Saviour God to Thee,
> How great Thou art! How great Thou art![5]

However, where there is no fear of Him, He has, and will, preside over His creation in judgement. "The Lord sat as king at the Flood; yea, the LORD sitteth as king for ever" (verse 10, RV; compare Psalm 18: 7-15). But Psalm 29 ends with a faithful promise for future Israel, "The LORD will give strength unto his people; the LORD will bless his people with peace!" (verse 11, RV).

PSALM 33: GOD'S WORD AND CREATION

Psalm 29 describes the immediate effects of the LORD's voice; Psalm 33 also celebrates the power of the LORD's word. Verses 1-5 call the saints ("the righteous") to praise the LORD, *firstly*, because His word is "upright" (verse 4); it has such moral power that "the earth is full of [His] steadfast love" (verse 5b). He made it; He has obligated Himself to it. In other places, The Psalms delight in "the steadfast (creatorial) love of the LORD" towards His creation, but especially towards the forgotten needy and disadvantaged of mankind. For example:

- "God ... the hope ["confidence", NKJV] of all the ends of the earth. ... You visit the earth and water it; you greatly enrich it. ... You crown the year with your bounty ["goodness", NKJV]" (Psalm 65:5, 9 & 11 – but read the whole Psalm!).

- "As a father shows compassion to his children, so the LORD shows compassion to those who fear Him. For he knows our frame; he remembers that we are dust. As for man, his days are like grass; he flourishes like a flower of the field; for the wind passes over it, and it is gone, and its place knows it no more. But the steadfast love of the LORD is from everlasting to everlasting on those who fear him, and his right-eousness to children's children" (Psalm 103:13-17).

- "Great are the works of the LORD, studied by all who delight in them. Full of splendour and majesty is his work, and his righteousness endures forever. He has caused his wondrous works to be remembered; the LORD is gracious and merciful. He provides food for those who fear him" (Psalm 111:2-5a).

- "The LORD is good to all, and his mercy ["tender mercies", NKJV] is over all that He has made. ... The LORD upholds all who are falling and raises up all who are bowed down. The eyes of all look to you, and you give them their food in due season. You open your hand; you satisfy the desire of every living thing. The LORD is righteous in all his ways and kind in all his works" (Psalm 145:9 & 14-17).

- "[The LORD] made heaven and earth, the sea, and all that is in them, who keeps faith forever; who executes justice for the oppressed, who gives food to the hungry. The LORD sets the prisoners free; the LORD opens the eyes of the blind. The LORD lifts up those who are bowed down; the LORD loves the righteous. The LORD watches over the sojourners; he upholds the widow and the fatherless, but the way of the wicked he brings to ruin" (Psalm 146:6-9).

- "He covers the heavens with clouds; he prepares rain for the earth; he makes grass grow on the hills. He gives to the beasts their food, and to the young ravens that cry" (Psalm 147:8-9).

Secondly, Psalm 33 calls on "the righteous" to praise the LORD because His word is all-powerful as well as upright. "By the word of the LORD the heavens were made, and by the breath of his mouth all their host" (verse 6, compare Psalm 148:4-6). He simply used *His word* to bring the creation into existence (compare Hebrews 11:3). What He commands is immediately accomplished and what He says stands fast (verses 6-9). As Psalm 68:33 declares, "[He] rides in the heavens, the ancient heavens; behold He sends out His voice, His mighty voice." The expressions "By the word of the LORD" and "by the breath of his mouth" in Psalm 33:6 underline the "God said .... And it was so" statements in Genesis 1;[6] and interpret them for us. The Genesis account means what it says. That is, the days are literal days. Psalm 33:6 states that He breathed the immense heavenly universe into existence, a fact that is echoed in Isaiah 40:26, "He who brings out their host by number, calling them all by name, by the greatness of his might, and because he is strong in power not one is missing" (compare Psalm 147:4-5).

Psalm 33:7 gives an interesting insight into Genesis 1:9-10. God is so great and powerful that He gathered the waters of the seas together as a heap [literally, "a wineskin", "bottle"]. The depths of waters were placed in storehouses, or treasuries, to be there for His own disposal, for example, at the Flood.

According to Psalm 33:9, "He spoke, and it came to be; he commanded, and it stood firm." But Hebrews 1:3 also says that the Creator (God's Son) continually *upholds* the entire creation by the word of His power. This echoes a truth that runs, if in other words, throughout the Psalms – in the sense that He is in total control of His creation, even over the greatest of land or sea creatures (e.g., Psalm 74:14 & Psalm 89:10). He also practically controls the environment, climate, and weather, so that His creatures have the resources to sustain them through life on earth (e.g., Psalm 36:6b below).[7]

Because of the omnipotence of the word of the LORD, Psalm 33:8 calls for all the earth to fear Him. And this introduces the *third* motivation for praise in this Psalm. So powerful a God "brings the counsels of the nations to nothing. ... Blessed is the nation whose God is the LORD, the people whom he has chosen for his heritage" (verses 10 & 12). But then, as now, the nations of the world do not fear Him (and as we saw in Chapter 1 they never have!) About these verses Derek Kidner comments, "[For the Psalmist,] to speak of nature's obedient glory is to be reminded of man's blatant defiance. It is not denied or minimised here, but it is looked at in the revealing context of "for ever" (verse 11). The standpoint of these verses is taken up and worked out at length in Isaiah 40 and following chapters (which is the best commentary on them) where "peoples" and their "counsel" come to naught or serve God's purpose unawares (e.g., Isaiah 44:25 and following verses; 45:4

and following verses), and where God's "chosen" (verse 12) are shown the searching implications of their call (Isaiah 41:8-20; 42:1; etc.)."[8]

But the LORD whose omnipotent *voice* brought all into being can by His omniscient *eye* properly assess everything "the children of men" do, because He individually constituted each of them and so understands them through and through (Psalm 33:13-15; compare Psalm 14:2-3). As a result, they have no power against Him (Psalm 33:16-17); and His eye, which assesses the hearts of the nations, also watches over those who fear Him and hope in His steadfast love (verses 18-19). So the Psalmist implies that His love is equal to His power. Yes, the Creator is also the Sovereign, the Judge, the Saviour and the Consummator! This steadfast love will be fulfilled in the Millennium, for which the believing soul waits (verse 20).

PSALM 36: HOW EXCELLENT IS THY LOVINGKINDNESS!

Like Psalm 33:5, verses 5 and 7 of Psalm 36 also celebrate the steadfast creatorial love of the LORD. In verses 5-6 David uses the grandeur of creation as similes of the moral greatness of God. His mercy (NKJV) is as immeasurable as the skies; His faithfulness is as high as the clouds; His righteousness is as immovable as the mountains; and His judgments are as unfathomable as the depths. Contemplating these makes this "servant of the LORD" (see title of Psalm) exclaim, "O LORD, You preserve man and beast" (verse 6b, NKJV). And this thought of the Creator's benevolence causes David to burst into praise in verse 7a (KJV), "How excellent ["precious", ESV] is Thy lovingkindness, O God!" David addresses "God" rather than "LORD", because all peoples, and not just the covenant nation, depend on their

Creator, and should also discover Him to be their Protector. And not only is there loving protection, but also fulness of supply, lasting satisfaction, joy, life, and light (verses 7b-9).

In verse 8, "the river of your delights [pleasures (NKJV)]" calls to mind the river coming out of Eden (Genesis 2:10-14); and anticipates the Millennial river-scene of Ezekiel 47 (compare Psalm 46:4; Joel 3:18 & Revelation 22:1). The Creator God continues to provide of His goodness for all of mankind throughout their entire history (compare 1 Timothy 4:10). David dwells on the greatness and goodness of God in conscious contrast to the arrogance and inventiveness of the wicked (verses 1-4). And so at the end He prays for that steadfast love [lovingkindness, NKJV] to continue to those who know Him, and His righteousness to the upright of heart, so that they do not fall victim to the arrogant rejecters of God (verses 10-12). A similar motivation for prayer occurs in 1 Timothy 2:1-5.

Chapter 8
The everlasting God, my Creator

In Chapter 7, I majored on the fact that The Psalms often celebrate that God is the only God and the sole Creator of all things. This chapter looks at some Psalms in which the thought of the immutable God personally impacted upon the Psalmist. "He who built all things is God" (Hebrews 3:4, NKJV). Christians take this for granted – so much so that it can make lamentably little impact on our thinking and lives. Not so for the writers of these four Psalms, whose words, therefore, can be described as the most basic of "reality checks".

PSALM 90: GOD ETERNAL; MAN TRANSIENT

Contemplation of God as Creator is closely linked to contemplation of His eternality. Moses composed this prayer for Israel to lament their wilderness wanderings after God's judgement came upon them (compare verses 7-9 with Numbers 14:20-35). As Moses contemplated the long years ahead for that generation of the nation, he was comforted by the fact that the disposition of every generation is in the hands of the Lord (verse 1; emphatic form of "Adonai" – "the Sovereign, the Owner"). But the ultimate answer to the nation's wanderings and homelessness was that He had been the saints' dwelling place [or "refuge", Septuagint] from the very beginning of time. "The eternal God is your dwelling place, and underneath are the everlasting arms" (Deuteronomy 33:27). Unlike us, God is not limited by the time and space He created. From eternity to eternity He is God (verse 2; "El" – "the Mighty One"), who had revealed Himself to Moses as the everlasting I AM (Exodus 3:14).

However, Moses can only trace back to the first days of creation. God precedes the birth of the mountains on Day Three of creation (Genesis 1:9-10); as He also of course pre-dates Day One! Perhaps verse 3 alludes to Genesis 3:19 and is filled out in verses 7-12, where God's wrath regarding man's sins has determined his expected lifespan. Yes, man is soon swept [flooded] away – his life no more than a passing dream, or grass that quickly grows and soon withers away (verses 5-6). Biblically, a thousand years is a very long time on man's timescale (compare Revelation 20:2-4), but it merely registers with God as a day or a night watch (verse 4, compare 2 Peter 3:8). What is our lifespan (verse 10) compared to God's eternality? To God, time is nothing (verse 2); He lives in eternity (Isaiah 57:15)! Moses recognises man's transience, "the years of our life are seventy, or even by reason of strength eighty; yet … they are soon gone, and we fly away" (verse 10). In these days, when men increasingly think that they are in control of the length their lives, we do well to pray, "So teach us to number our days that we may get a heart of wisdom" (verse 12).

PSALM 102: THE ONE WHO ABIDES FOR EVER AND IS 'THE SAME'

Psalm 90's theme also runs through Psalm 102. Here the Psalmist's own experience of human frailty sharpens his sense of God's eternality. He prays as "One afflicted, when he is faint and pours out his complaint before the LORD" (Psalm title). Verses 1-11 elaborate his distress, Just when his life is ebbing away (verse 11), he turns from self-occupation to his God and exclaims, "But you, O LORD, are enthroned for ever; you are remembered throughout all generations" (verse 12). His cry becomes more intense as death draws ever nearer, "[God] has broken my strength in midcourse; he has shortened my days. 'O my God,' I say, 'take me not away in the midst of my days'" (verses 23-24a). Mid-sentence, the Psalmist changes to addressing God as Creator, "you whose years endure throughout all generations!" (verse 24b). He now sees his own transience from the perspective of God's overall plan for the entire creation. "Of old you laid the foundation of the earth, and the heavens are the work of your hands. They will perish, but you will remain; they will all wear out like a garment. You will change them like a robe, and they will pass away, but you are the same, and your years have no end" (verses 25-27). The N.Tr. renders "the same" in verse 27, "the Same",[1] with an explanatory footnote, "… a name of God [meaning], 'The existing One, who does not change.'"

In contrasting the brevity of his own life with the unchangeability of God, the Psalmist finds consolation in the fact that His purposes regarding Zion are unchangeable too (verses 12-22). However Hebrews 1:10-12 applies verses 25-27 directly to Christ *the Son* as one of the proof-texts of His essential deity "without even a comment being deemed necessary."[2] The whole Psalm is Messianic and gives an insight into the Lord's prayers in Gethsemane.[3] The title, together with verses 1-11 and verse 23, express the extremity of His grief. Verse 10 gives the reason, "because of your indignation and anger". His prayer in verse 24 is interrupted by the Father's ready response of verses 24b-27, reminding Him, "thou art the Same" (verse 27, N.Tr.). J.N.Darby comments, "The Christ, the despised and rejected Jesus, is Jehovah the Creator. The Ancient of days comes, and Christ is He, though Son of man. This contrast of the extreme humiliation and isolation of Christ, and His divine nature [i.e., as the Creator], is incomparably striking."[4]

But it is through this One, "the Afflicted" (title) but now set at God's right hand, the One who *Himself is* the unchangeable God, that the promises regarding Zion will be fulfilled (verses 13, 16 & 21-22 with Jeremiah 31:12 & 33:14-16).

PSALM 104: CELEBRATION OF THE CREATOR AND ALL HIS WORKS

This celebration is the Psalmist's own, personal response as he considers his God manifest in His many acts both at creation and in His ongoing involvement with creation. In musing over the Genesis account of creation, the Psalmist composes poetry by which his soul can bless the LORD.

The praise exhibits a striking, if general, correspondence to the days of the Creation Week.

- Verses 1-4 introduce the Creator in all His divine majesty and awesome power.
  - Verse 2a mentions light, which came on Day One (Genesis 1:3-5).
  - Verse 2b extends light to include the formation of the starry universe, created on Day Four (Genesis 1:16b).

94

- Verses 3-4 explain how God operates in the heavens He formed on Day Two (Genesis 1:6-8).

- Verse 5 introduces the earth which is the focus of the remainder of the Psalm and indicates God's special interest in it.

- Verses 6-9 recall how the Creator separated the land from the seas on Day Three (Genesis 1:9-10), so that the earth could be inhabited.

- Verses 10-18 laud the provision of water for the earth to allow vegetation, plants and trees to spring forth, so that there is food and drink for all creatures including man. This also commenced on Day Three (Genesis 1:11-13).

- Verses 19-23 recall the divine appointment and design of the sun and the moon to govern the seasons, days and nights, and years, which happened on Day Four (Genesis 1:14-19).

- Verses 24-26 rejoice in the profusion of creatures on the land and in the seas, which were created on Days Five and Six (Genesis 1:20-25). The description is prefaced by a special note of praise, "O LORD, how manifold are your works! In wisdom have you made them all" (verse 24a).

- Verses 27-30 give poetic voice to Genesis 1:29-31, extolling the dependence of all creatures, terrestrial and aquatic, upon the Creator for life and death, for sustenance and safety. (This theme is taken up again in Psalm 107, with the appropriate response of verse 31, "Let them thank the LORD for His steadfast love, for His wondrous works (including the storms of verses 23-30!) to the children of men!").

- Verses 31-35 provide a fitting finale of glory and praise from the Psalmist (and from us also!) to the

Creator; and they correspond to Day Seven, the Sabbath (Genesis 2:1-3).

PSALM 139:13-18: YOU MADE ME!

For David, life in essence is "God and me". In verses 1-6, the *omniscient* God knows and sees everything in David's life; in verses 7-12, the *omnipresent* God is always there with him through all of life, and even in death (compare Psalm 23:4); whilst verses 19-24 teach the *all-righteousness* of God. But in verses 13-18, David confesses that his God, the omnipotent One, is the Creator who personally made him as an individual!

Verse 13 declares, "You formed my inward parts; you knitted me together in my mother's womb."

- The design and begetting of a human life (i.e., of you and me!) is God's work alone, even though your/my parents were involved! God is intimately involved with every human being from the very start of his/her existence. Conception, the formation of the foetus of a baby, and its ultimate birth are profound mysteries, which science does not and cannot explain (either the How? or the Why?) – even with a knowledge of DNA!

- In this verse, "formed my inward parts" is literally, "possessed my kidneys." "Possessed" implies that God is Lord. The NIV translates verse 13 as, "You created my inmost being", on the grounds that the "kidneys" represent the seat of our desires and longings, our moral compass, our inner motives, the things which God tests (compare Jeremiah 17:10).[5] God is "Lord" of these.

- "Knitted" means "intricately woven together" as a complex unity. "Your hands have fashioned and made me. …You have made me like clay. … You clothed me with skin and flesh, and knit me together with bones and sinews" (Job 10:8-9 & 11).

- "In my mother's womb" means that a foetus is a real person from conception!

No wonder David says in verse 14, "I praise you, for I am fearfully and wonderfully made. Wonderful are your works; my soul knows it very well."

- "Fearfully" means "I am to be in awe of [hold in reverence]" the specialness of my body.
- "Wonderfully" [or, "marvellously"] is a comment upon the complexity of the human anatomy.
- Each person is made differently – is unique!

David continues in verse 15, "My frame was not hidden from you, when I was being made in secret, intricately woven in the depths of the earth."

- "My frame" means "my skeleton".
- "In secret … in the depths of the earth" is a Hebrew idiom for the deepest concealment and intimacy of the process of procreation.
- "Intricately woven" is "embroidered" (similar in meaning to verse 13) showing that each part of the human anatomy is curiously fashioned by God; this "fashioning" is the secret behind what we now know is the human genome.

"Your eyes saw my unformed substance" (verse 16a) confirms that the embryo is designed and known by God.

- In Hebrew, "unformed substance [or, body]" is "embryo". The human embryo medically is the first eight weeks from conception.

- "Unformed" is translated 'unperfect" by RV and KJV, giving the idea of not fully developed, yet possessing life from God!

- Fundamentally, life is sacred because it comes from God![6]

"In your book were written, every one of them, the days that were formed for me, when as yet there was none of them" (verse 16b). How blessed to understand that God has His special plan for the exact number of days for your/my life (and also for the life of every other person) from conception to death (or to the Lord's coming)! And so, like David, we confess, "How precious to me are your thoughts, O God! How vast is the sum of them! If I would count them, they are more than the sand. I awake, and I am still with you" (verses 17-18).

CHRIST'S BY CREATION AND REDEMPTION!

LORD, we are *Thine*: our God Thou art;
Fashioned and made we were, as clay;
These curious frames, in every part,
Thy wisdom, power, and love display;
Each breath we draw, each pulse that beats,
Each organ formed by skill divine,
Each precious sense aloud repeats
Great GOD, that we are only Thine.

LORD, we are *Thine*: in Thee we live,
Supported by Thy tender care:
Thou dost each hourly mercy give –
Thine earth we tread, we breathe Thine air
Raiment and food Thy hands supply,
Thy sun's bright rays around us shine;
Guarded by Thine all-seeing eye,
We own that we are wholly Thine.

Lord we are *Thine*: bought by Thy blood –
Once the poor guilty slaves of sin;
Thou hast redeemed us unto God,
And made Thy Spirit dwell within;
Our sinful wanderings Thou hast borne
With love and patience all divine:
As brands, then, from the burning torn,
We own that we are wholly Thine.

Lord, we are *Thine*: Thy claims we own –
Ourselves to Thee would humbly give;
Reign Thou within our hearts alone,
And let us to Thy glory live;
Here may we each Thy mind display,
In all Thy gracious image shine;
So shall we hail that looked-for day,
When Thou shalt own that we are *Thine*.[7]

Chapter 9
Creation's hallelujah-crescendo!

In the overview to Part 4, I stated that some Psalms include a celebration of the creatorial power that will introduce the glorious rule of Messiah. But it is in the final six Psalms (145-150) that creation's "hallelujahs" are concentrated. For Christian believers "hallelujah" is the language of saints who anticipate, and in the future participate in, "the kingdom of our Lord and of His Christ".[1] In this respect, the praise of the books of Psalms and Revelation coalesces. However this chapter highlights the ways in which these "Hallelujah Psalms" celebrate the blessed reign of the Creator over His restored creation. Then, as now, the One who determined the number of the stars binds up the broken-hearted (Psalm 147:3-4). What a cold and empty universe, by contrast, the atheist imagines he inhabits! By contrast the last six Psalms express the praise that all creation ought always to give to its Creator.

PSALM 145

Each of the Psalms 146-150 starts and finishes with the refrain, "Hallelujah" or "Praise the LORD"; however their grand finale of praise to the Creator flows out of Psalm 145. This Psalm is entitled "David's Psalm of praise" in the KJV. J. M. Flanigan has written, "… 'Psalm of praise' is a translation of one Hebrew word. This is, literally, 'David's praise', or, 'David's Praise-Song' and no other Psalm has this word in its title. Psalm 145 is all praise. … It is therefore a fitting introduction to … 'The Hallelujah Psalms'. … The closing verse of Psalm 144 seemed to anticipate the kingdom, [so] now the King Himself is extolled."[2] As David's last attributed Psalm, it consummates all his personal worship found in his other Psalms, "My mouth shall speak the praise of the LORD" (Psalm 145:21a, NKJV).

Psalm 145 is full of hope of Jehovah's rule, for example, verse 13a, "Your kingdom is an everlasting kingdom, and your dominion endures throughout all generations." And it extols the greatness (verses 1-7), the goodness (verses 8-10), the glory (verses 11-13), the providence (verses 14-16), and the saving grace (verses 17-21) of David's "God and King", as David addresses Him in verse 1.

Psalm 145 is the last alphabetical Psalm,[3] and so it is a complete[4] acrostic of praise from David, the "sweet Psalmist of Israel", whose prophetic vision of the Creator present upon earth was of "One [who] rules justly over men, ruling in the fear of God, he dawns on them like the morning light, like the sun shining forth on a cloudless morning, like rain that makes grass to sprout from the earth" (2 Samuel 23:1b & 3-4).

Not only does the Psalmist himself praise, but so do restored Israel in each ensuing generation throughout the entire Millennium (verse 4). They triumphantly praise and laud the LORD because they know their

Creator, and have first-hand experience of Him. They know all about Him – all His majesty, His awe-inspiring acts, His ever-flowing, abundant goodness, His ability to establish and maintain righteousness, His grace and His tender mercy (verses 5-9). But above all they appreciate His abundant steadfast love [great loving-kindness, N.Tr.] (verse 8b).[5]

Every part of His creation ("all that he has made", verse 9) benefits from His presence and responds appropriately with thanksgiving (verse 10a). However His saints are able to bless Him (verse 10b); and they speak of the glory of His kingdom and tell of His power, making Him known to the children of men throughout the entire globe (verses 11-12). The result, "the earth shall be full of the knowledge of the LORD as the waters cover the sea" (Isaiah 11:9 & Habakkuk 2:14). And there will be universal acceptance of the sovereign Creator; "Your kingdom is an everlasting kingdom, and your dominion endures throughout all generations" (verse 13a). When this occurs all David's desires are satisfied, "May the whole earth be filled with his glory! Amen and Amen! The prayers of David, the son of Jesse, are ended" (Psalm 72:19-20).

Psalm 145:14-20 suggest that David also recognised what dependence on the Creator's constant benevolence will mean in practical terms. Throughout the Millennium, there will be:

- Help for the vulnerable (verse 14).

- Food for all creatures (verses 15-16).

- Speedy answers for those who pray (verses 18-19).

- Total preservation of those who love Him (verse 20).

David concludes his meditation on Messiah's rule with thoughts that the praise will outlast the Millennium (and the end of time) and will continue into eternity.[6] "My mouth will speak the praise of the LORD, and let all flesh bless his holy name forever and ever" (verse 21, compare verse 1).

> At length, the final kingdom
> No bound, no end possessing,
> When heaven and earth
> God all in all
> Shall fill with largest blessing:
> All root of evil banished;
> No breath of sin to wither;
> On earth, on high,
> Nought else but joy
> And blissful peace for ever.[7]

PSALM 146

The praise of Psalm 146 contrasts dependence upon man – of whatever status (verses 3-4) – with the blessedness of the one whose help and hope are in "my God" (verse 2). As a godly Israelite, the Psalmist personally appreciates His grace as revealed by the name the "God of Jacob" (verse 5a). Like Jacob, he has come into the blessedness of God's faithfulness. His hope is in his God, who is "the LORD ... who made heaven and earth, the sea, and all that is in them" (verses 5-6a, compare Psalms 115:15, 121:2, 124:8 & 134:3). The Creator is the compassionate One who has sovereign rights that are both judicial and moral (verse 7). Hence the praise repeats the themes of justice, providence, saving grace and tender mercy found in Psalm 145:6b-9. It also resembles Psalm 145 in that it climaxes with the enduring praise of the everlasting reign of the LORD (verse 10). Therefore the repetition of the opening refrain, "Praise the LORD!"

PSALM 147

Psalm 147 invites re-gathered *Israel* to praise their God (verses 1-2 with verse 12), who is at once identified as the great and powerful Creator (verses 4-5, 8, 14-18). He is the tender Protector of them, His new-covenant people, "who hope in his steadfast love"[5] (verses 2-3 & 6 with verse 11).

Verse 4 says He is the same One who determined the number of the stars and named all of them! (Compare Isaiah 40:26-31.)

Verses 8-9 arise from a second invitation to praise (verse 7) and include praise/thanks for His providential care for all His creatures (including the ceremonially unclean ravens!) via the natural food cycle. His providential care is executed by His creatorial control of the elements (snow, wind and water) and their seasonal variation through the means of His commanding, powerful word (verses 15-18). But to restored Israel He gives peace and prosperity – "the finest of wheat" (verse 14) – as He promised the nation as they entered the land (Deuteronomy 32:14 & Psalm 81:16).

Therefore the invitation to "praise the LORD" is renewed in verse 12, with verses 13-20 listing reasons for it. Most of all, Israel's special relationship with Jehovah includes the privileges of knowing (and propagating) His written word (verses 19-20 with 145:11-12). Hence the final refrain, "Praise the LORD!"

But notice that verse 1 announces that praise is good, pleasant and fitting for the people of God (including us!) whenever they fear Him, that is, accept His all powerful wisdom. It sets their hope in Him, their trust in His steadfast love[5] (verse 11).

PSALM 148

Psalm 148 commands *universal* praise, that is, praise from the heavens and the earth (compare Psalm 69:34). We know from Romans 8:19-22 why such praise will rise during the millennial reign of Christ.

Verse 4 is an echo of Creation Day Two when the heavens were formed (compare Nehemiah 9:6); and the "waters above the heavens" suggest the re-establishment of Edenic climatic conditions.

Verses 5-6 of this Psalm state why heavenly bodies (verse 3) and heavenly beings (verse 2, compare Psalm 29:1-2) can praise the LORD. It is because He is their Creator, their Controller, and their Sustainer. "Let them praise the name of the LORD! For he commanded and they were created. And He established them forever and ever; he gave a decree [that is, "law of nature"] and it shall not pass away" (verses 5-6).

Verses 7-14 invoke praise from the planet earth – the seas and all in them; all the elements of nature; mountains and hills; plants, animals and birds; as well as from all peoples of both sexes, whatever their status or age (compare Psalm 103:21-22).

In verses 11-13, the whole of mankind is required to raise an adequate "hallelujah chorus". But verse 14 says it is the saints who are especially enabled to praise, "the people of Israel who are near to him."

- W. G. Scroggie states, "The choice of Israel is regarded as having a central and universal significance for the whole life of creation. This is not the view of any historians except the Biblical, but the whole revelation of the Bible rests squarely on the fact."[8]

- J. N. Darby comments, "The great Creator whom heaven and earth must praise is the God of Israel, and Israel His people."[9]

Israel are the people called by Jehovah's Name (2 Chronicles 7:14). It is the excellence of Jehovah's Name and His transcendent majesty (compare Psalm 8:1) that generate praise from earth (verse 13).

PSALM 149

Psalm 149 arises out of Psalms 146 & 148, and anticipates the Millennium by commanding the "new song,"[10] in which revived Israel shall rejoice in their Maker with joyfulness and gladness of heart (verse 2). This ecstatic praise is expressed both publicly and in private (compare verses 3b & 5b), and is elaborated upon in Psalms 93 & 96-100. The children of Zion rejoice in their long-awaited King (Psalm 149:2). However, according to Psalm 147:20, this rejoicing also occurs when the nation awakes up to the privileges of its vocation (compare Psalm 110:3). But the new song can only be maintained throughout the world of mankind on the basis of divine righteousness; therefore Psalm 149:6-9 remind Israel to be the effective instrument of God's government (compare Isaiah 26:9). The Psalm ends with a resounding hallelujah of victory!

PSALM 150

Psalm 150 is the grand finale both of these "hallelujah Psalms" and of the entire Psalter. It is a fitting doxology from "everything that has breath" to its Creator (verse 6). It is the actual realisation of the hopes and aspirations in Messiah that are expressed in all the prophetic Psalms.

Verse 1 tells *who* will be praised – the LORD ("Hallelu-Jah") who is also God ("Hallelu-El"). It also tells *where* He will be praised during the Millennium. He will be praised in the sanctuary of the temple, which is His chosen dwelling-place upon earth in Jerusalem, the capital of Israel and the metropolis of the world (compare Exodus 25:22 with Ezekiel 48:35). But His praise extends to the whole universe and fills His mighty heavens.

- Derek Kidner remarks, "Earth and heaven can be utterly at one in this. His [creatorial] glory fills the universe; His praise must do no less."[11]

Verse 2 explains *why* He will be worshipped – for what He does through His mighty acts of creation (compare Psalm 33:6-9) and salvation (compare Psalm 106:8-10). He is also praised for His excellent greatness (Psalm 150:2b; compare Psalm 8:1) because He is the Creator and the Sovereign.

Verses 3-5 state *how* He will be praised. It will be with all the instruments that are used in Israel's temple worship.

Verse 6 answers the question, "*by whom* shall He be praised?" Its invitation is, "Let everything that has breath [that is, every living creature which breathes][12] praise the LORD!" (verse 6a).

- Derek Kidner comments that verse 6a, "is literally, 'Let all breath praise the LORD'. ... The glorious variety [of life] that was glimpsed in Psalm 148:7-12, with 'sea monsters ..., beasts and all cattle, creeping things and flying birds', joined by the whole family of man from kings to children – indeed, as Psalm 8:2 declares, to babes and sucklings."[13]

Praise the LORD!

Conclusion

O Lord! How long?

Many Psalms anticipate the personal intervention of the Creator to restore His creation to Edenic conditions. Their general focus is on Messiah's global reign. "For the Lord, the Most High, is to be feared, a great King over all the earth" (Psalm 47:2). However, as Christian believers we must finish our study of creation Psalms with the wider prophetic view afforded by Psalm 8 – namely, of Christ as the Son of Man set over all creation, and ruling in both heaven and earth (compare Ephesians 1:10 & 22). Meanwhile, like the godly in the Psalms (e.g., Psalm 90:13 & Psalm 94:3) we cry out, "O Lord! How long?" For we, too, know that lasting righteousness, peace, prosperity and blessing on earth for mankind await the Christ's everlasting kingdom (see Chapters 10 & 11).

> Come, blessed Lord, bid every shore
> And answering island sing
> The praises of Thy royal name,
> And own Thee as their King.
>
> Bid the whole earth, responsive now
> To that bright world above,
> Break forth in rapturous strains of joy
> In memory of Thy love.

Lord, Lord, Thy fair creation groans,
The air, the earth, the sea,
In unison with all our hearts,
And calls aloud for Thee.

Come, then, with all Thy quickening power,
With one awakening smile,
And bid the serpent's trail no more
Thy beauteous realms defile.[1]

Part 5
Creation
to come

Chapter 10
Creation Restored

God's perfect creation has been spoiled by sin. But did God fail? Impossible! The intention of Eden will be realised in The Millennium (Revelation 20:3, 5, 7). We can call the creation that was commanded and formed into being in Genesis 1:1 – 2:24 the "old" creation, because we know God has a new one coming (Revelation 21:1)! In time to come, He will make "all things new" (Revelation 21:5), as we will find out in Chapter 12.

When God made the "old" creation, it is recorded that at the end of each of Days Three to Five, "And God saw that it was good" (Genesis 1:12, 18, 21). In the middle of the Sixth Day also, after making the land creatures other than man, "And God saw that it was good" (verse 25). Then when He had made man, the apex of His creation, "And God saw everything that He had made, and behold, it was very good" (verse 31).

But, as was discussed in Chapter 3, it did not last that way for very long! Genesis 3 recounts how, through the disobedience of that very apex of His creation (man), sin entered the world "and death through sin" (Romans

5:12). The entrance of sin brought in corruption and death (Romans 8:20-21). Since then, and up to now, Satan, sin, and death have been permitted to defy God in the "old" creation. But, in the new, righteousness will "dwell" unchallenged, and God will be "all in all" (2 Peter 3:13 & 1 Corinthians 15:25-28).

So is this "old" creation just going to be "written off" as a failure? Not at all! God has no failures; He is going to win! All that the Devil defiled and sin corrupted is going to be restored! In the Millennial Kingdom of God, and before God brings in His new creation, the Devil will be restrained and all enemies, except death, defeated (Revelation 20:1-3 & 1 Corinthians 15:24-26). Edenic conditions will first return (e.g., Isaiah 35:1-2 & 6-7) before this "old" creation is done away – not in disgrace or judgment, but as a garment which has served its purpose (e.g., Isaiah 51:6 & Hebrews 1:10-12). So much so, that in some respects "new creation" language can be used of this "old creation" when it is restored in those wonderful coming days.

NEW CREATION IN ISAIAH – THE ORIGINAL CREATION RESTORED

This is why the prophecies of Isaiah climax by the Lord GOD declaring, "Behold, I create new heavens and a new earth, and the former things shall not be remembered or come to mind" (Isaiah 65:17). Most Bible translations provide marginal cross-references at Isaiah 65:17 to 2 Peter 3:13 and Revelation 21:1. But these are texts that deal with the "real" new creation, the creation that will succeed this one. And the context and internal evidences of Isaiah 65-66 point rather to the Millennial Kingdom of the Lord Jesus Christ. This can be verified by comparing and contrasting Isaiah 65-66 with Revelation 21:1-9:

- Isaiah's centre is still the original earthly Jerusalem; and her people, Israel, are still claimed by Jehovah to be "my people" (65:18-19; 66:8-10, 13 & 22-24).

  - In contrast to this, Revelation 21:3 (describing new creation) applies the symbolic meaning of Jerusalem to the church, which is both new and heavenly (compare Galatians 4:25-26).

- Isaiah 65:20 states that death, although perhaps exceptional, can occur.

  - However, death is expressly said to be "no more" in the description of new creation in Revelation 21:4.

- In Isaiah 66:23, the times, seasons and Sabbaths established in Genesis 1:14-19 & 2:1-2 remain continuing features of life.

  - But these are among the "former things" that in Revelation 21:4 are said to have passed away (compare Galatians 4:3, 9-10).

Nevertheless, many of the moral and spiritual characteristics of the Millennial Kingdom that will come "in power" at the public advent of our Lord from heaven will foreshadow those of the ultimate "new creation", or what is called the "eternal state":

- It will be characterized by righteousness. Throughout The Millennium, righteousness will reign – "reign", because enemies will still need to be held down (Jeremiah 23:5-6 & 1 Corinthians 15:25). The Lord Jesus Christ will reign as King of kings and Lord of lords. "Behold, a king will reign in righteousness, and princes will rule in justice" (Isaiah

32:1). Isaiah 65:17-25, along with Isaiah chapters 11-12, 35 & 60-61, describe the effects of the Messiah reigning out of Zion (compare Joel 3:17-18).

- It will be a most blessed time. Other Scriptures, such as Psalm 72 & Zechariah 14, present the benefits of Messiah's worldwide rule for the whole world.

- This entire creation, which is currently under bondage and groans for that time (the time of the revealing of the sons of God), will be liberated (Romans 8:19-22).

- It will come under the glorious dominion of the Son of Man – see Chapter 11 about Psalm 8, which prophetically celebrates His universal reign.

- People will also be changed physically; great longevity of life will be the norm (Isaiah 65:20-24).

- Daniel repeatedly prophesied that the Millennial Kingdom will be an everlasting kingdom, that is, never to be superseded and enduring until the end of time (compare Daniel 2:44; 4:34-35; 6:26; 7:13-14 & 27 with 2 Peter 1:11).

- Original and creatorial relations will be re-established as the Creator makes a covenant with the rest of creation on behalf of His covenant people (Hosea 2:16-23). Restored Israel will be in a proper new-covenant relationship with Him on the basis of "the blood of [his] covenant with [them]" (Zechariah 9:11). It will be a relationship as sure as the LORD's powers to maintain His creation (Jeremiah 31:31-37). No wonder Paul describes this future period for Israel in new-creation terms as "life from the dead" (Romans 11:15)!

In summary, during the Millennial Kingdom, the world will benefit from much that is *new*:

- A new spirit, the Holy Spirit (Isaiah 32:15-16 & 44:3).

- A new morality resulting in ongoing fairness, righteousness and peace (Isaiah 2:3-4, 11:4-5 & 32:17-18; Micah 4:1-5).

- A new universal government, with Jerusalem its administrative centre (Psalm 72:8; Isaiah 9:6-7; Jeremiah 3:17).

- A new economy centring on Jerusalem (Isaiah 60:17 & Zechariah 14:14).

- A new climate (Isaiah 30:26 & 60:19-20).

- A new topography (Ezekiel 47:8 & Zechariah 14:4, 10).

- A new distribution of flora and fauna (Psalm 72:16; Isaiah 32:15, 35:1-2 & 6-7, 55:13; Ezekiel 34:25, 47:8-12 & Joel 3:18).

- A new zoology (Isaiah 11:6-9, 65:25 & Hosea 2:18).

- A new husbandry (Amos 9:13).

And it will be a world *without*:

- Idolatry – for God will be known and acknowledged throughout the whole world (Isaiah 11:9; Habakkuk 2:14 & Zechariah 14:9).

- Want – for everyone will have plenty (Psalm 72:16; Isaiah 27:6; Jeremiah 31:12-14 & Amos 9:13-15).

- War and violence – for there will be worldwide peace (Isaiah 2:4; Micah 4:3 & Zechariah 9:10).

- Injustice and oppression – for Christ will rule in absolute righteousness (Psalm 72:12-14; Acts 17:31 – based on Psalms 9:8 & 98:9).

- Fear and threat – for there will be safety and total security (Micah 4:4; Zechariah 2:4-5 & 8:5).

- Confusion – for Babel will be undone (Zephaniah 3:9).

- Disease, disability, sickness (Isaiah 33:24 & 35:5-6).

- Dangers disasters, destruction, difficulties (Genesis 12:3 & 22:18; Jeremiah 4:2; Isaiah 35:8-10 & 65:19).

- The Devil's influence (Revelation 20: 1-3).

All in all, these conditions are so different from the world that Isaiah experienced and that we currently experience, that "new" is an appropriate description of the restored creation. The Creator Himself effects all these changes when, at His Appearing, He cleanses all of the corruption and contamination of man's sin, especially that from the Great Tribulation period. "The *glory* of the LORD shall be revealed, and all flesh shall see it together, for the mouth of the LORD has spoken" (Isaiah 40:5 with my emphasis). No wonder that "the creation awaits with eager longing" (Romans 8:19) for the coming kingdom!

But it is a *kingdom*, that is, an exercise of righteous authority; and it has a purpose, namely that *every* enemy be put down (1 Corinthians 15:24). The Devil, who has been under total restraint during the Millennial Kingdom, will be released at the end of it "for a little while" (Revelation 20:3) to demonstrate that unregenerate man is basically no different from what he ever was since the Fall. But Satan's rebellion will be summarily crushed; and he himself finally judged. Then will come the Great White Throne judgment, and "Death and Hades", too, will be "cast into the lake of fire" (20:7-15). The "last enemy" will have been destroyed. The whole purpose of this enormous history of Creation will have been realised, namely that *all* the glory of destroying all evil will belong to God's self-emptying, incarnate, self-sacrificing and risen Son *alone* (1 Corinthians 15:24-26).

Then it will be time to introduce the New Creation – see Chapter 12.

Chapter 11
Christ, the Son of Man set over all Creation

Chapter 9 concluded a survey of Creation Psalms by
pointing out the wider prophetic view afforded by
Psalm 8 – namely, of Christ as the Son of Man set over
all creation, and ruling in both heaven and earth (compare Ephesians 1:10 & 21-22). To find out the truth
about the name or title, "Son of Man", we must study
Psalm 8 in the light of the New Testament, for it shows
how the LORD/Jehovah, by being made truly Man, and
dying, rising and ascending, set His own glory above the
heavens. That glory will be displayed in the world to
come (Hebrews 2:5-8). David asks (verse 4, NKJV),
"What is man that You are mindful of him, and the son
of man that You visit him?" It is a question about the
special nature and character of mankind – why does
mankind mean so much to God? To paraphrase, "Why
should an all-powerful God be mindful of [literally
"remember", "be compassionate for"] mortal man; why
should He visit [literally "care for", "attend to"] man even
in all his dignity, seeing that He is so great?"[1] The ultimate answer is that God has always had in mind His

Anointed One, the Man of all His counsels (Ephesians 1:11).

ADAM – FROM THE HAND OF GOD

As a shepherd, David must have spent his night watches contemplating the moon and the stellar heavens with their galaxies. He looked up (verse 3) and saw their vastness (how bad that nowadays there is, so we read, too much light pollution in most of Britain to see what David saw, even through telescopes!). Looking around (verses 6-7), and down into the seas, as well as up (verse 8), David reflected on the majesty and glory of God in creation, and recognised it to be all the work of the LORD's fingers (verse 3). In astonishment, he states that man is not an insignificant, unnoticed speck in the vastness of the universe, but rather the crowning act of God's creation! In verses 5-8 he elaborates the complete answer (as far as Old Testament truth revealed) to the question he asked in verse 4. Yes, Adam was made in God's image. He is God's representative – man with all his potential; man in all his dignity, dominion and destiny (Genesis 1:26-31). A man who "was made a little lower than God" (ESV footnote and AMP) is the literal Hebrew of Psalm 8:5. Sadly Adam fell into sin and forfeited his unique position!

Creationists have correctly emphasised the 'Anthropic principle'.[2] This is the scientific evidence that the whole universe is precisely designed and operated to support life and, uniquely, mankind; and it is evidence that God made it for Adam and Eve. However, Scripture emphasises that the universe exists primarily for the *last Adam*, or the *second Man*, our Lord Jesus Christ, the Man in whom there is no failure. Romans 5:14 (NKJV) asserts that Adam "is a type of Him who was to come." So, to make the link between "Son of man" and Christ, we must consider the whole of Scripture, not just Genesis 1; only then can we fully answer David's question, "What is man?"

"And so it is written, 'The first man Adam became a living being.' The last Adam became a life-giving spirit. However, the spiritual is not first, but the natural, and afterward the spiritual. The first man was of the earth, made of dust; the second Man is the Lord from heaven" (1 Corinthians 15:45-47, NKJV).

FALLEN MAN

Old Testament writers seem perplexed about the character of man. Job poses the same question as David. He asked if man could ever be right with God, especially as he noticed that all people were continually scrutinised by God (Job 15:14, 25:6 & 7:17-18). David again asked, "What is man?" in Psalm 144:3-4, because he recognised that all people are under judgement; they are both mockers and opposers of God and the godly. David and Job just saw mankind in all its puny frailty: the "man" they considered was only feeble, mortal man, only *enosh!*[3]

In reality, the answer to "What is man?" awaited the advent of Christ.

JESUS CHRIST, THE SON OF MAN ON EARTH

The Lord quoted the Septuagint version of Psalm 8:2 to justify the children praising Him in the temple precincts. "Out of the mouth of babes and nursing infants You have perfected praise" (Matthew 21:16, NKJV). More importantly, almost without exception, He claimed the title "Son of Man" for Himself.

Godly Jews, understanding the Hebrew idiom, would appreciate that "Son of Man" meant that Jesus Christ was truly a Man in every sense of the word. (In Hebrew, "son of ..." implies "having the character of ...") Luke's Gospel highlights our Lord's *Manhood*: and Luke's genealogy of Him shows His descent ("as was supposed") from both *Enosh* [mortal man], and *Adam* [man made by the finger of God] (Luke 3:23, 38). But I must hasten to add that with Jesus there was none (that is, not one!) of those defects that Job and David had identified in mankind. Christ was a Man totally without sin, and apart from sin (Hebrews 4:15; 1 John 3:5). He "knew no sin" (2 Corinthians 5:21).

Almost one-third of the Lord's references to Himself as the "Son of Man" focus on the closing events of His life: His rejection, humiliation, sufferings, and death. He became Man in order to die, and when He spoke about Himself as "Son of Man" He was effectively committing Himself to the pathway of the cross. "And he began to teach [the disciples] that the Son of Man must suffer many things, and be rejected by the elders and the chief priests and the scribes and be killed, and after three days rise again" (Mark 8:31). Like those disciples, we must allow these words to sink into our ears and hearts (Luke 9:44), for His death is life for us (John 6:53).

Another one-third of the Lord's references to Himself as the Son of Man relate to His second coming. For example, "But in those days, after that tribulation, the sun will be darkened, and the moon will not give its light, and the stars will be falling from heaven, and the powers of the heavens will be shaken. And then [everyone] will see the Son of Man coming in clouds with great power and glory" (Mark 13:24-26). At His trial, the Lord warned the high priest, "I am [the Christ, the Son of the

Blessed] and you will see the Son of Man seated at the right hand of Power, and coming with the clouds of heaven" (Mark 14:62). (Notice that Caiaphas *did* see Him! It was through Stephen, when the latter exclaimed to the Sanhedrin, "Behold, I see the heavens opened and the Son of Man standing at the right hand of God" (Acts 7:56).) "Behold, he is coming with the clouds, and every eye will see him, even those who pierced him, and all tribes of the earth will wail on account of him. Even so. Amen" (Revelation 1:7). God the Father also has given Him authority to judge, because He is the Son of Man (John 5:27).

CHRIST JESUS, THE EXALTED SON OF MAN

But already at this present time Jesus, "is seated at the right hand of the throne of the Majesty in heaven" (Hebrews 8:1). The statement at the end of Psalm 8:6, "you have put all things under his feet," is used three times in the New Testament epistles to substantiate several truths of Christianity in which the supremacy and dominion of the Son of Man are of paramount importance.

First of all, Hebrews 2:5-10 quotes and explains Psalm 8:4-6. The Son of God became the Son of Man in order to suffer death for everything (Hebrews 2:9, N.Tr.). Whilst, at present, not everything is in subjection to Him, we do see Him at God's right hand (compare Psalm 110:1, also Hebrews 1:3 & 13, 8:1, 10:12 & 12:2). In Hebrews 2:9, He is "crowned with glory and honour", with the writer alluding to the Septuagint version of Exodus 28:2 regarding Aaron's "holy garments ... for glory and for beauty." Hebrews 2:6 quotes David's question in Psalm 8:4 (NKJV), "What is man that You are mindful of him, and the son of man that You visit him?"

Hebrews 2:8b onwards answers David's question by showing that God's care for man is found for believers in the high priestly grace of the Lord Jesus Christ.

Secondly, the statement from Psalm 8:6 is quoted in Ephesians 1: 22, "And he put all things under his feet". This occurs in the context of verses 20-23, in which Paul enumerates five things that God the Father has done in relation to The Christ. Using the aorist, the tense which shows that these things have already been completed, Paul asserts that:

- God worked in the [dead] Christ and
- He raised Him from among the dead.
- He seated Him at His own right hand in heavenly places.
- He put all things under His feet – Lordship.
- He gave Him to be head over all things to the church – Headship, especially in the sense of the "chief".

Here we see a meaning in Psalm 8:6 that could not be revealed until the ascension of Christ! Ephesians 1:9-10 expands upon Psalm 8:1, and states that all things on earth and in heaven will be headed up in The Christ. This is the "secret of God's will"! Everyone in those times will see Him, and He will be "far above all rule and authority and power and dominion, and above every name that is named, not only in this age but also in [that age] to come" (Ephesians 1:21). Yes, we Christian believers know that Christ, The Son of Man, will be set over all creation because we see Him in this present dispensation in all His glory, the Man at God's right hand in heaven!

Thirdly, the statement from Psalm 8:6 is also quoted in 1 Corinthians 15:27, "God has put all things in subjection under his feet." This occurs in a section (verses 20-28) which describes the unstoppable march of resurrection in its chronological sequence from Christ's own resurrection to the end of time and into eternity.

- Verses 20-23 say that Christ as Man is the Guarantor that everyone belonging to Him (all who are "in/ belong to Christ") will be raised to life immortal. He is the Victor over death itself (verse 26)!

- Notice that death is described in verse 26 as man's last enemy. It outlasts the Millennium and is finally dealt with by the Son of Man at the Great White Throne Judgment of all who are spiritually dead (Revelation 20:7, 11-15). Then time ceases and the first creation passes away. Immediately John's vision is of eternity, where "death shall be no more" (Revelation 21:4 with verses 1-8, which describe the "eternal state"). 1 Corinthians 15:54 describes death's demise in resurrection terms, "When the perishable puts on the imperishable, and the mortal puts on immortality, then shall come to pass the saying that is written: 'Death is swallowed up in victory.'"

- Verse 57 triumphs, "But thanks be to God, who gives us the victory [now] through our Lord Jesus Christ." However, the victory song has already been celebrated in verse 27, where Psalm 8:6 is quoted. The "all things" of the quotation were already detailed in verses 24-25 – "every rule", "every authority and power"; and "all his enemies." Yes, Christ, The Son of Man will be supreme over all creation in the restored creation!

- Verses 45-49 powerfully make, both by similarity and contrast, the link between Adam and Christ that is essential to the interpretation of Psalm 8:

- the first Adam ("a living being [or, soul (foot-note)]") and the last Adam ("a life-giving spirit"), verse 45

- the natural and the spiritual, verse 46

- the first man and the second Man, verse 47

- the man of dust and the Man of heaven,[4] verse 48

- we have borne the image of the man of dust; we shall also bear the image of the Man of heaven, verse 49.

Whereas none of the epistles uses the actual title/name of "Son of Man" (except by quotation in Hebrews 2:6), it occurs again in Revelation where prophetic issues and future judgements resurface. Christ is first symbolically seen in this book in the midst of the seven lampstands [that is, amongst the seven churches in Asia] as, "One like the Son of Man, clothed with a garment down to the feet and girded about the chest with a golden band" (Revelation 1:13, NKJV). This reminds us of Peter's admonition in 1 Peter 4:17, "For it is time for judgment to begin at the household of God; and if it begins with us, what will be the outcome for those who do not obey the gospel of God?" The end of the disobedient is described in Revelation 14:14-20, when the Son of Man executes judgements upon the earth; and, again at the Great White Throne Judgment (Revelation 20:11-15). Of the Son of Man, Daniel 7:13-14 says, "To him was given dominion and glory and a kingdom, that all peoples, nations, and languages should serve him; his dominion is an everlasting dominion, which shall not pass away, and His kingdom one which shall not be destroyed."

THE UNIVERSAL REIGN OF THE SON OF MAN

The three allusions to Psalm 8 in the Epistles tell us that the Psalm celebrates the universal reign of the Son of Man, God's True Representative, as set over all the works of God's hand and ruling the whole of restored creation. As we saw in Part 4, this is the prophetic objective of the whole book of Psalms. If we regard Psalms 1-8 as an overall 'Introduction to The Psalms', then Psalm 2 introduces the Messiah established in Zion in *the last times of world-wide opposition to God* (also echoed in Psalm.8:2, "because of your foes") and emphasises Christ's royalty as the anointed King (Psalm 2:6, N.Tr.) with "the nations [his] heritage, and the ends of the earth [his] possession" (Psalm 2:8). Psalm 8 exults in the majesty and supremacy of His universal Kingdom. Notice, again, that verse 9 repeats verse 1, "O LORD, our Lord, How majestic is your name in all the earth!" But in verse 1, the scope of Jehovah's majesty [N.Tr.] extends both "throughout all the earth" and "above the heavens" (compare Hebrews 2:5-10, Ephesians 1:20-23 & 1 Corinthians 15:20-28 above). David was meditating upon the majestic Name and glory of the LORD/Jehovah, the Name that describes who He is – the great I AM (compare Exodus 3:14-15)! But Jesus is Jehovah the Saviour (Matthew 1:21), whom God has made both Lord and Christ (Acts 2:36). Israel's hope, and God's plan for mankind, will be fulfilled in the Millennial reign of the Lord Jesus Christ over the entire universe. When He sits in majestic glory and reigns over all the earth as the Son of Man, all David's desires are fulfilled and he worships (compare Psalm 72:18-20)!

1 Corinthians 15:27 states that only God is excepted from Christ's supremacy during His Millennial reign.

The Kingdom is consummated when all things are brought into subjection to Him, and death, man's last enemy, is destroyed (verse 26). Though in Godhead co-equal with the Father, the Son of God then subjects Himself as Son of Man to God the Father for all eternity; and the eternal state, in which "God (Father, Son and Holy Spirit) is all in all", comes to pass (verse 28).

> LORD, what is man? 'Tis He who died
> And all Thy nature glorified,
> Thy righteousness and grace displayed
> When He for sin atonement made,
> Obedient unto death, was slain –
> Worthy is He o'er all to reign.
>
> Thy counsels ere the world began
> All centred in the Son of Man,
> Him destined to the highest place,
> Head of His church through sovereign grace.
> To Him, enthroned in Majesty,
> Let every creature bend the knee.
>
> Worthy, O Son of Man, art Thou,
> Of every crown that decks Thy brow;
> Worthy art Thou to be adored
> And owned as universal Lord;
> Oh, hasten that long promised day
> When all shall own Thy rightful sway![5]

Chapter 12
And finally, New Creation!

Any book on creation must conclude with a chapter about new creation. F. B. Hole reflected this approach in his book, *The Great Salvation*, and emphasised its importance when he wrote, "We have left "new creation" until the last [chapter of the book] as it seems to be the ultimate thing to which the Gospel conducts us, but at the same time it is evident that God is going to establish it, not because it meets some definite need on our side, but because it meets the need of His holy nature – it is the thing which is suitable to Himself."[1]

This means that the present creation (including the restored creation in the Millennial Kingdom of God) is merely a necessary precursor, a platform for God to work out the counsel of His will to achieve His eternal purpose. In a little over one thousand years from now the creation we now live in will have worn out. "Thou in the beginning, Lord, hast founded the earth, and works of thy hands are the heavens. They shall perish, but thou continuest still; and they all shall grow old as a garment, and as a covering shalt thou roll them up, and they shall be changed" (Hebrews 1:10-12, N.Tr.). But the new creation is eternally "new in character" (Greek word: *kainos*) rather than "just recent", that is, "new in time". It will never decay; rather it abides forever!

NEW CREATION IN DISTINCTION TO THE ORIGINAL CREATION RESTORED

It is true that the Old Testament writers sometimes described as a "new creation" the Edenic conditions of Christ's Kingdom, when this present creation will be restored. But it must be emphasised this is different to what the apostle John wrote of in Revelation 21:1-8. This contrast was pointed out in Chapter 10. As Hebrews 12:26-29 makes clear, everything "that has been made", that is, the entire material universe, will be consumed by fire, leaving only that which endures for eternity (compare 2 Peter 3:10-13).

BEHOLD, I MAKE ALL THINGS NEW!

Following his vision of the final judgment of mankind in Revelation 20:11-15, John sees a new heaven and a new earth in the new vision of 21:1-8. The first heaven and earth have passed away. 2 Peter 3:10-12 explain that they will be burnt up and dissolve in the judgment. Revelation 21:1 ends with the statement, "and the sea was no more",[2] suggesting that nothing will disturb or trouble the eternal state of bliss in which God dwells with man (verse 3). The vision emphasises things belonging to this present groaning creation which will all be absent. Tears, death, mourning, crying and pain all will be no more (compare Romans 8:22-23). Unlike in the Millennium, righteousness will not need to reign in the new creation, for there will not be even the potential for sin (compare Revelation 21:8). Righteousness will dwell there (2 Peter 3:13). God Himself will have His dwelling-place [or, tabernacle] with men (verse 3).

For us, this will involve the tender and intimate touch of a loving Father. "God will wipe away every tear from [his people's] eyes" (verse 4a). Nevertheless it will be commanded from His throne, "Behold, I am making all things new" (verse 5).

In verses 2-3, the Church is brought into focus as:

- "The holy city" – it bears the nature of God, consistent with our holy calling (compare 2 Timothy 1:9 with Ephesians 1:4 & 2:21).

- "The new Jerusalem" – not the old earthly, literal city, but a city in figure that symbolises the home of the heavenly saints (compare 3:12).

- "From God" – it is divine in origin.

- "Out of heaven" – in its character as well as its location (compare Hebrews 3:1).

- "A bride adorned for her husband" – prepared to belong to Christ for eternity, the object of His eternal love (compare Ephesians 5:25-27).

  - Revelation 21:9 – 22:5 present a different vision of the Church, which, as the Lamb's wife, rules with Him over both heaven and earth in the Millennium (compare Ephesians 1:9-11 with Revelation 21:24).

- The eternal "dwelling place of God", the culmination of that which is true of us even now in time, "In [Christ] you also are being built together into a dwelling place for God by the Spirit" (Ephesians 2:22).

Notice that the Church is the product of God's new creation work, "that he might create in himself one new man in place of the two, so making peace, and might reconcile us both to God in one body through the cross.

... In [Christ Jesus] the whole structure, being joined together, grows into a holy temple in the Lord" (Ephesians 2:15-16 & 21).

THE BEGINNING OF THE CREATION OF GOD

We know that God began by creating the heavens and the earth on Day One of the creation, and that He completed this creation when He created Adam and Eve last on Day Six (Genesis 1:1 & 26-31). God breathed into man the breath of life (2:7). But the new creation *starts* with the Man, the Christ, whom God raises out from among the dead to new life (Ephesians 1:20-22 & Romans 6:10). In Revelation 3:14 Christ is called "the beginning of the creation of God" (KJV), echoing the Name assigned to Him in reference to His resurrection in Colossians 1:18-19, "He is the head of the body, the church. *He is the beginning [of the new creation]*, the firstborn from the dead, that in everything he might be pre-eminent. For in him all the fullness of God was pleased to dwell" (my expansion and emphasis). This description of Him immediately follows verses 15-17, where He is identified as the Creator and Sustainer of this present creation. Therefore in God's new creation, which is both established in and maintained by the risen Christ, He is also the pre-eminent One.

"IN CHRIST" THERE IS NEW CREATION NOW!

According to 2 Corinthians 5:17 believers already belong in a spiritual way to the new order of new creation, "Therefore, if anyone is in Christ, he is a new creation. The old has passed away; behold, the new has come." Verses 15-21 of 2 Corinthians chapter 5 present seven facets of this doctrine of new creation *now*:

- Every believer is a new creation because he/she is seen by God as being "in Christ" (verse 17, compare Ephesians 2:10). Ephesians 1 explains in detail what it means for believers to be "in Christ," and highlights that their election was according to the eternal purpose of God.

- "Behold, the new has come" (verse 17). As new creatures "in Christ", all believers experience new creation realities now! New birth has given us new life, a new beginning, with new desires, new aspirations, and a new hope. 2 Corinthians 4:4-6 draws a comparison between God's new-creation work of shining into our hearts and His old-creation work of commanding the physical light to shine out of the darkness (Genesis 1:3). In Genesis 1:2-3 the Spirit of God and the word of God conjointly produced the natural light, and thereby they pictured the work of God when a person is born anew into the kingdom of God (John 3:3 & 5, N.Tr.). However, in new creation the light-source is the face of Jesus Christ, and the shining is the glory of God!

- "Old things have passed away; behold all things have become new" (verse 17, N.Tr.). In the death of Christ, God has put away everything pertaining to our old life (Romans 6:4, 6 & Colossians 2:11-14).

- "From now on, therefore, we regard no one according to the flesh ..." (verse 16). Our relationships are transformed by our transforming relationship with the Lord Jesus.

- Everything is from God (verse 18), and designed by Him for His own satisfaction and pleasure (compare Revelation 21:3).

137

- God accomplished new creation through His righteous work of reconciliation. "For our sake he made him to be sin who knew no sin, so that in him we might become the righteousness of God" (verse 21). In the new creation, *all things*, which were all tainted by sin in the old creation (compare Job 15:15 with Hebrews 9:23-24), will be made new, and finally and totally reconciled to God (Colossians 1:20).

- God brings in new creation "through Christ" (verse 18). Verses 14-15 speak of His love, His death, and His resurrection, and their subjective effect upon us. If His death be regarded as the womb of new creation, then His resurrection is the birth of new creation.[3] But "through Christ" also means that, spiritually, new creation is even now maintained for believers in the power of His endless life and the permanency of His priesthood (Hebrews 7:16 & 24). We are "all of one" with Him in His risen manhood (Hebrews 2:11, KJV).

NEW CREATION IN ACTION

"For neither circumcision counts for anything, nor uncircumcision, but a new creation" (Galatians 6:15).

According to Galatians 6:14-16, real piety concerns the manifestation of my new life "in Christ Jesus" (Galatians 5:6). Everything in Christianity is about "walking by this rule," namely, the rule of my old self having been crucified and replaced by Christ living in me with my accompanying walk in the Spirit (Galatians 2:20 & 5:24-25).

Colossians 3 exhorts, "If then you have been raised with Christ seek the things that are above, where Christ is seated at the right hand of God. Set your minds on things that are above not on things that are on earth. ...

Put to death therefore what is earthly in you. ... Put off the old self with its practices and have put on the new self, which is being renewed in knowledge after the image of its creator. ... Here [in new creation] ... Christ is all, and in all" (verses 1-2, 5 & 9-11 with my expansion).

Ephesians 2:8-10 says we were saved to be God's "workmanship, *created in Christ Jesus* for good works, which God prepared beforehand, that we should walk in them" (italics added). The Greek word for workmanship, *poiēma*, is translated "the things that have been made" in Romans 1:20. If God's physical creation displays His eternal power and divine nature, our new-creation "good works" manifest His grace and love. As members of Christ's body, we express Him to the world by walking in these good works, which are elaborated upon in Ephesians 4-6.

THEN COMETH THE END

Although God started His new creation in the resurrection of Christ, His first creation continues until the end of the Kingdom. "Then comes the end, when [Christ] delivers the kingdom to God the Father after destroying every rule and every authority and power" (1 Corinthians 15:24). The context of this verse describes the unstoppable course and consequences of the resurrection of Christ (1 Corinthians 15:20-28). Time started in Genesis 1:1, but ends when "God [is] all in all" (1 Corinthians 15:28). At that point, He, the One seated on the throne declares, "Behold, I make all things new" (Revelation 21:5, NKJV). Immediately, Christ declares about the *physical* new creation, "It is done! I am the Alpha and the Omega, the beginning and the end" (Revelation 21:6, compare Revelation 1:8 & 22:13).

The apostle Peter explains how the first creation terminates. "The heavens will pass away with a roar, and the heavenly bodies will be burned up and dissolved, and the earth and the works that are done on it will be exposed" (2 Peter 3:10). Then in verses 12-13, he says that these final judgements introduce the day of God, or the eternal state, in which righteousness will dwell in the new heavens and new earth. This is our destiny, and since we are, *even now*, spiritually God's new creation in Christ, it follows that our conduct in this present world must comply with Peter's admonitions of 2 Peter 3:11-14, "Since all these things are thus to be dissolved, what sort of people ought you to be in lives of holiness and godliness, waiting for and hastening the coming of the day of God. ... Therefore, beloved, since you are waiting for these [new heavens and new earth], be diligent to be found by him without spot or blemish, and at peace."

And in relation to our destiny in the new creation, we read something incomparable in 1 Corinthians 15:28. "When *all things are subjected to him*, then the Son himself will also be subjected to *him who put all things in subjection under him*" (italics added). Notice the strong emphasis on Psalm 8:6 in the italicised clauses, emphasising that in 1 Corinthians 15:28, just as in verse 27, Christ is still viewed as Son of man. Yet verse 28 directly refers to the Lord in His greatness as "the Son" to show that what is about to be stated is not at all what one would have expected. The Son will be "subjec*ted*" to God (the KJV's "be subject" is wrong; He will not be subjugated). This verse proves that the Son is not intrinsically subject to the Father; if He were, He would not need to be subjec*ted*. But even One so great as the co-equal Son will *voluntarily* subject Himself as Son of man to God *for ever*. Having taken manhood upon

Himself out of love for His Father and love for us, He is never going to abandon it. He says, in the Old Testament picture, "I love my master, my wife and my children; I will not go out free" (Exodus 21:5). He remains the risen Man throughout eternity, as well as being "God blessed for ever" (Romans 9:5); for ever the Man who is Head over all things to His Church, and Husband to His bride (Ephesians 1:22-23 & Revelation 21:2). And the object of His lovely action is "that God [Father, Son and Holy Spirit] may be *all in all.*" The Trinity, alone in its untouchable glory, will for ever be utterly distinct from every creature. But at the same time our creaturehood is established eternally in new creation by the Son Himself remaining the risen Man for ever with all who are raised with Him (compare Hebrews 2:11). What a wonderful thought!

EXHORTATION AND DOXOLOGY

"But grow in the grace and knowledge of our Lord and Saviour Jesus Christ. To him be the glory both now and to the day of eternity. Amen" (2 Peter 3:18).

Part 6
Creation
Postscript

Chapter 13
Creation and Science

SCRIPTURE VERSUS SCIENTIFIC THEORIES

In the Introduction to this book, I made clear that it would *not* primarily be about the 'creation versus science' issue. However, many people think that science has replaced the Bible as *the* authority on everything to do with life, matter and the universe. It is especially the current scientific theories on the origins of the universe and life itself which are cited as major objections for people to believe the Gospel. This attitude was reflected in Radio 4's programme, 'A history of the future', broadcast 14 September 2012. It considered Leonardo da Vinci, who it described as both a man of God and a scientist – and in that order! It said that because he knew from Scripture that his entire life would be scrutinised at the Judgment, with heaven or hell as an eternal destiny, he ensured that his science always honoured his Creator. It then contrasted this approach to science with twentieth-century science, which challenges not only whether God is the Creator of the universe, but also whether or not He really exists. Yet, Leonardo da Vinci was not unique. In fact, many of the early scientists were God-fearing men. For example, Kepler described his scientific investigations as "thinking God's thoughts after Him". I must also emphasise that there are many genuine Christian believers amongst today's scientists.

Scientific theories occur to the inventive minds of scientists. These inventive minds are also reprobate minds (Romans 1:28, KJV) if these scientists are unregenerate men. Whatever odd circumstance may have made a scientist think of his or her theory, the scientific method demands it to be tested against reality, in order to distinguish the useful (no amount of testing can ever prove a theory to be finally "true") from the useless. However, even in the practice of present-day scientific testing, data from actual experiments is sometimes falsely interpreted; and theories are believed to be supported by evidence which, in fact, is inconsistent with them. The less exact the testing that is possible, the more the room for the accepted theories to be shaped by the hidden biases, preconceived ideas, and agendas of the inventive minds that imagined them, rather than by the evidence. No one can deny that the underlying urge to eliminate God from His universe has been a powerful propellant of macro-theories of the origins of life and the universe. The real issue is, as Leonardo da Vinci appreciated, if there is no Creator who made me, I can live as I please because there is no prospect of any future judgment from a holy and a righteous God.

THE THINGS THAT ARE

Believers have put their faith in the Scriptures. This means we accept the revelation of God about the origins of life and that the universe was created from no pre-existing materials. "And it is after all only by faith that our minds accept as fact that the whole scheme of time and space was created by God's command – that the world which we can see has come into being through principles that are invisible" (Hebrews 11:3, Phillips). After quoting this verse from KJV, Colin Curry wrote in 'The Heart of Christianity',

"It is a commonplace matter [of fact] that persons like ourselves have *being*. Yet the fact that anything at all *exists* has its own major significance. Efforts to "explain" physical reality apart from the Bible have ranged from quite fanciful ideas long since abandoned, to the more disciplined and reasonable-sounding notions currently in vogue. The biblical answer to this question stands apart from all the rest, however. It lies in the realm of revelation from God. The others are the product of human searchings and speculation. Moreover, the biblical answer is the only real answer. Other explanations are always tentative (including the up-to-date ones). They depend on processes of *theorising*, and sooner or later they lack facts to support them. An "answer" which ultimately relies on pure speculation hardly deserves that status. "Science has all the answers" is a common thought with many people, but the proper scientific spirit is less confident, and knows its limitations. Science (properly so called) *can* account for many things; it can *describe* processes in the physical realm and in some measure it can *understand* the dynamics of what goes on in given situations. But origins, discontinuities, the boundaries between non-existence and existence, are entirely outside its province. The sudden emergence, from nothing at all, of an all-comprehensive embryo of the universe (matter, or energy, in some unimaginably potent form) is no truly

scientific explanation. It is in fact an utterly naïve idea.
The belief that everything that *is* consists of a complete
"going concern" all on its own, without some ground of
being behind it, is a naïve faith indeed. As an answer it
begs all the questions. The biblical understanding of
these fundamental questions also comes by faith, but
faith of this kind has much to support it. Resting on
God, the God of the Bible, the God of revelation, it is
indeed a well-grounded faith.

According to the Bible, things as they *are* provide the
first stage of God's witness to Himself. Their very existence speaks of Him. In them His voice is heard, and His
glory declared. Persons and things exist, and are a
standing testimony to a fount of life and being outside
of themselves. All other supposed understanding in this
area falls short of real understanding. It comes close to
pure credulity, it is a cover for ignorance, it is preference
for darkness. These are strong statements, but they indicate what the Bible teaches. The very fact that I can say
"I am" rebukes my folly if I ignore God. Doing so, I have
turned away from something which faces me firmly and
unequivocally. Of course the voice of God in creation is
greatly reinforced by further disclosures from Himself.
The voice of Scripture is the Word of the living God; it
is alive with His authority and vitality. Human awareness of moral standards (and of shortcomings in the
light of those standards) indicates strongly that there is
a world of eternal values and judgments consonant with
the character of God. It also provides special evidence
that man is a distinct part of God's handiwork. All these
voices to men supplement the testimony of creation to
God. Above all else, there is "the true light, which (having come into the world) shines for every man" (John
1:9). The most conclusive of all witnesses to God has

shone in Christ, and continues to shine. Nothing can add to that! How comprehensive is the whole story of God's revelation of Himself to men!

To sum up the immediate point of the present section [of my book], however, persons and things have *contingent existence*, not existence in their own right. Our very being is a pointer to the living God "in whom we live and move and have our being". [He is] 'The God that *is*'. "He that cometh to God must believe that He *is*, and that He is a rewarder of them that diligently seek Him" (Hebrews 11:6)."[1]

THE SCIENCE I PRACTISED

Ever since my schooldays, I have always found science fascinating. After qualifying, I fulfilled my ambition to become an analytical chemist. For ten years, I worked in the quality control laboratory of a manufacturer of Active Pharmaceutical Ingredients (APIs), also known as Drug Substances. For any practising chemical analyst, it is necessary to provide results which accurately reflect the intrinsic quality of the product. With respect to APIs, there is an addition ethical reason for this – the product is a medicine! This is achieved by using authentic methods of analysis performed with calibrated equipment by suitably qualified and trained analysts. The validation of the analytical method is essential (technical words such as: specificity, accuracy, precision, ruggedness, linearity, system suitability, etc., all apply). Every scientist knows the limitations of the measurement she/he uses for whatever determination; and that extrapolation beyond the proven range (the linearity, or straight line of the graph) cannot provide a reliable result. The extremes of extrapolation are guesswork. Therefore, as a scientist, I am very sceptical of the data used by geological scientists (for example, test results on the age of rocks); and of other scientists who propose non-Biblical theories for origins.

After ten years, I changed to the demanding role of quality management (in the pharmaceutical industry this is known as good manufacturing practices, GMP). As with other chemical manufacturers, API manufacturers must exercise responsible care for the environment and for the health and safety of their employees (and neighbours). In addition, GMP requires them to be ethical – their products, which are complex organic compounds or biological entities, must be therapeutically beneficial to patients, nothing more and nothing less! Legal requirements demand records must be made and kept to demonstrate that every batch of product actually has been manufactured by the validated process (the process proven by laboratory trials) to give the correct product at the (very pure) standards required for medicinal use. This is achieved by using high-quality starting materials in the process and by carrying out the process within the proven acceptable ranges for the critical parameters. In my experience (over 40 years), whenever these conditions have not been followed, the 'reaction soup' never yielded the desired product (at best, an impure product; at worst, a tar!). I also know that investigating situations where conditions were outside the proven ranges (deviations) is very challenging, even with a good batch record. Root cause analysis is always difficult for any scientist!

Part of my company's activity was with chiral chemicals[2] and later in my professional life I encountered peptide, polypeptide and oligonucleotide chemistry[3] ... so I know that the constituent parts of DNA are extremely

150

difficult for any chemist to make, even under strict laboratory scale conditions with proper supervision (intelligent input) by highly qualified chemists; and that these products so easily degrade (decay) in normal/ prevailing environmental conditions.

In conclusion, from my involvement in these types of chemical manufacture (where GMP standards are based upon the best scientific practices) I know that chemical evolution[4] is impossible! Therefore, whatever critical statements I make in the next two chapters about the science of origins, I also make as a scientist as well as a Christian who believes in the inerrancy of the word of God. And I am not alone in my views; many other scientists, including some who are not believers, are similarly critical of the science of origins.

Chapter 14
Creation versus the scientific hypothesis of Evolution

WHAT? EVOLUTION YOU CAN BELIEVE IN!

During the 1960s a recently-saved teenage friend of mine was studying A-level sciences, which included biology because he wanted to become a pharmacist. But he objected to being taught that life simply "evolved". One chemistry-lesson experiment demonstrated that when aqueous acid is added to a carbonate salt solution an effervescence of carbon dioxide gas results. Upon producing this effect his science teacher exclaimed, "There you are, Chapple! Evolution you can believe in!" Using the word "evolution" in the different but correct sense of the bubbling of gas from out of a liquid,[1] the teacher was exactly right in pointing out that for scientists, testing, seeing and recording leads to the establishment of fact (belief). Until the mid-twentieth century, those who challenged the scientific validity of evolutionary biology were tolerated, as the teacher's light-hearted pun shows. However, nowadays evolution is aggressively promoted as scientific truth.

But the theory of biological evolution cannot be satisfactorily tested by experiment to show that it actually works; a point I shall return to below. Nor has it ever been observed to happen, despite what biology textbooks state about the peppered moth, for example! (Earlier claims that this species of light-grey moths "evolved" into black moths in response to the increasing deposits of soot in nineteenth-century London have given way, in the latter half of the twentieth-century, to the [reluctant] acceptance that black moths were already present, if rarely, in the moth population. In fact, with the 1956 & 1968 Clean Air Acts, consolidated into the 1993 Clean Air Act, the light-grey variety again predominates.) Rather, evolution is something scientists have faith in – in the same way that we believers have faith in God. As Edgar Andrews astutely observes, "The problem I have is that evolution can always contrive an answer…and can therefore never be falsified. Yet the capacity for falsification is essential for any truly scientific theory. So pervasive is the belief that *evolution can be the only truth*, that today it is simply assumed."[2] Andrews, formerly professor of material sciences at Queen Mary College, University of London, is making the point that evolution is infinitely inventive on explaining away difficult observations. For example, it purports that the exquisite beauty of the peacock's tail is due to mating competition. But how does one peacock impress a peahen rather than another? Also, this idea is directly contradicted by evolution's main hypothesis, survival of the fittest, which suggests that something as cumbersome as the peacock should be extinct by now in a world full of predators. But be sure some evolutionist will have an "explanation" for this as well! This type of reasoning makes evolution an article of faith, rather than a testable scientific hypothesis.

So we can say that evolution is the god of naturalism and secular materialism. Humanists need evolution *in order* to be able to dispense with the thought of God, so that they do not need to glorify Him as God, and give thanks. Because humanity refused to glorify Him as God "they became futile in their thinking" (Romans 1:21). In consequence God gave them debased, or degenerate, minds (Romans 1:28). Ever since, they have been alienated from God; and at enmity with Him in their minds [thinking] (Colossians 1:21). As I said in Chapter 13, this thinking leads to the deluded conclusions that there are no absolute morals and that there is no prospect of any future judgment from a holy and a righteous God.

FROM MICRO TO MACRO?

It is indeed a true and repeatable scientific fact that the addition of aqueous acid to a carbonate salt solution produces an effervescence of carbon dioxide. This kind of science could be called "operational science", and it is the basis of all modern-day technology, which has been such a benefit to mankind. (For example, commercial medicinal salts preparations contain citric acid and sodium bicarbonate powders to produce the effervescence of carbon dioxide when they are dissolved in water.) Operational science describes processes that work and that we know from experience to work (our modern way of living depends upon them working, time after time!). Operational science that interprets information from the natural world can only produce "best-fit" descriptions of reality, as we readily see in weather forecasts. Although the data usually comes from experiments or observations, sometimes the conclusions reached are incorrect (for example, climate change). And, with the exception of its established laws,

results are at best tentative and the theory is always subject to change if/when the science advances (this is
technically known as the law of radical change). What is
scientifically deemed to be 'true' today may be classified
as 'false' tomorrow!

But there is also a species of theoretical science which
uses current observations of the natural world to
extrapolate outside the limits of the present-day
(known) data-ranges into remote past ages and thus
attempt to explain the history of the universe.[3] For this
reason, claims that the hypothesis of evolution has been
proved experimentally are irrelevant. A Spanish Ph.D.
geneticist I once met exemplified the extrapolation just
mentioned. "But evolution does work!" he protested
when in discussion with me. He had researched genetic
variations in human populations and therefore had
proof of *micro evolution*. This is the scientific name for
the small changes which manifest themselves *within*
populations of given species. It is the result of natural
variation and selection within the species, but everyone
knows this has boundaries! Macro evolution, however,
is the proposal that all life originated from the same
micro organisms in a "primeval soup", and that these
then, by random mutations (infinitesimal chance
changes) over millions of years, developed from simple
organisms to an almost innumerable variety of complex
species!

But this has not been supported by "accelerated" muta-
tional testing of fruit flies. For all the laboratory
breeding of fruit flies to examine genetic mutations
under varieties of (extreme) circumstances, everything
that has resulted has still been a fruit fly! By now evolutionary scientists have had the time to breed over two
thousand generations. Also, over 30,000 generations of

E. coli bacterium (equivalent to about one million human years) have been studied with the E. coli remaining unaffected.[4] By extrapolating micro-evolutionary facts to prove macro-evolutionary claims, facts get mixed up with unproven hypotheses; and two very different issues are presented under the one generic name of "evolution".

WHAT SAITH THE SCRIPTURE?

Macro evolution is inconsistent with Scripture, so that Bible believers can say that evolution is *refuted* by Scripture. Notice the repetition of the phrase, "according to their kind", in Genesis 1 for all plant life and all trees (verses 11-12); all sea creatures and all birds, including all flying creatures (verse 21); all creatures and all animals (verses 24-25). Each kind was created separately, that is, there is no gradual development from simple to complex organism or from lower to higher form. 1 Corinthians 15:38-39 emphasises this truth, "God gives [the sown seed] a body as he has chosen, and to each kind of seed its own body. For not all flesh is the same, but there is one kind for humans, another for animals, another for birds, and another for fish."

And, as believers, we know from Scripture that man *did not* evolve from lower life-forms, for Genesis 1:26-29 states that mankind, both male and female, was God's special creation. David in Psalm 8:4 ponders over this issue, and asks the question (my paraphrase), "Why is man so special?" Psalm 8:5-6 provide answers by referring back to Adam (Genesis 1:26-29 & 2:4-7). In reality every individual is specially created by God, a fact David appreciated, "You formed my inward parts; you knitted me together in my mother's womb" (Psalm 139:13). Similarly Elihu declares, "The Spirit of God has made me, and the breath of the Almighty gives me life. … I too was pinched off from a piece of clay" (Job 33:4 & 6). Job understood that such knowledge gave him a moral conscience to care for his servants. He asks in Job 31:15, "Did not he who made me in the womb make [them]? And did not one fashion us in the womb?"

And in 1 Corinthians 12:18, Paul wrote about the human body, "God arranged the members in the body, each one of them, as he chose." W. E. Vine comments on this verse, "—this states the perfect will, the flawless plan of the almighty and all-wise Creator. The placing of the members exhibits unity but not uniformity. Moreover, the tenses of both verbs are the aorist or point tenses … and this marks the formation of [each] human body in all its parts as a creative act at a single point of time, and contradicts the evolutionary theory of a gradual development from infinitesimal microcosms."[5] About verse 24, "God has so composed the body, giving greater honour to the part that lacked it", Vine continues, "the emphasis is on "God," and the force of the statement is this: "it was God who tempered (or blended) the body together." And the natural instinct which fulfils what verse 23 states is God's doing."[5] No wonder David says, "I praise you, for I am fearfully and wonderfully made. Wonderful are your works; my soul knows it very well" (Psalm 139:14).

WHERE DID LIFE COME FROM?

We also know from Scripture that life *did not* begin by chance from an inorganic ('ordinary chemicals') "primeval soup". (Molecular evolution is the term now used for this abiogenesis, that is, the alleged emergence of the living cell from non-living materials. Evolutionary scientists know that it is contradicted by the law of biogenesis, and *wilfully* choose to ignore the issue!) Scripture asserts that it was God, the source of all life, who gave life to the plants and animals and to mankind (Genesis 1:11-13 & 20-25, 2:7). Job asks, "Who among all these [creatures] does not know that the hand of the LORD has done this? In his hand is the life of every living thing and the breath of all mankind" (Job 12:9-10). This fact is scientifically confirmed by the law of biogenesis, which was discovered and confirmed experimentally by Louis Pasteur in 1861. It states that *"life must come from life"* The central truth of the Gospel is that Jesus Christ is the Creator God incarnate. Science is silent over this fact – and it also cannot explain either His miracles or His resurrection from among the dead! It is John's Gospel which introduces Him as the Light of the World, "In him was life, and the life was the light of men" (1:4). In Scripture, light shows what things really are, that is, *light is the knowledge of reality.* John introduces his Gospel in 1:1, "In the beginning was the Word, and the Word was with God, and the Word was God." The Lord Jesus Christ is personally the Word of God, the One fully capable of expressing who God is. Verse 18 goes further by stating He has fully made God known to men. Life for every human being is conscious existence. Reality then is to know where natural life came from – it came from God, the Source of all life, speaking it into the creatures He made and breathing it into Adam.

LIFE OUT OF DEATH

One biological definition of livings things is that they die! But death is not an inherent feature of life, a hangover from the process of evolution; it is the direct consequence of Adam's disobedience at the Fall. "Sin came into the world through one man, and death through sin, and so death spread to all men because all sinned" (Romans 5:12). Because Adam had dominion over all creation, it, too, came under the bondage of corruption (Romans 8:20-21). Romans 5:19-21 states the good news of salvation, "For as by the one man's disobedience the many were made sinners, so by the one man's obedience [unto death] the many will be made righteous…so that, as sin reigned in death, grace also might reign through righteousness leading to eternal life through Jesus Christ our Lord." The Gospel brings the hope of life beyond the grave, life beyond the reach of death, through the resurrection of the Lord Jesus Christ from among the dead. Hallelujah!

ETERNAL LIFE

The Lord Jesus Christ came to bring that which is true life to those who believe on Him (John 10:10). That life is called eternal life in the New Testament. Spiritual reality is to have eternal life, the knowledge of God the Father (the only true God) and His Son, Jesus Christ (the Sent One, the Revealer of God) (John 17:3). 1 John 5:11-13 testifies that Christian believers are confident they know God through His Son and have been brought into *ultimate reality, called eternal life.* Verses 19-20 describe it in these words, "We know that we are from God … And we know that the Son of God has come and has given us understanding, so that we may know him who is true; and we are in him who is true, in his Son Jesus Christ. He is the true God and eternal life." About which a spiritual mentor of mine used to say, "Yes, we know that we know that we know! Sadly, unbelievers don't know that they don't know that they don't know!"

CHAPTER 14

CONCLUSION

In conclusion, 'science' ought to recognise that it does not know everything. Rather, the more science discovers, the more complicated physical realities are shown to be. So complex are living organisms that for life to start spontaneously (as described by the hypothesis of evolution) that John C Lennox has shown it to be impossible in terms of mathematical probability – it is more than $10^{40,000}$ to 1![6] But the surgeon Dr Vij Sodera goes further in his book *One Small Speck to Man* and asserts, "The evolution of one type of creature into a different type of creature *did not* occur, and *cannot* and *will not* occur under any circumstances ... *ever*". Hence the subtitle of his book, *The Evolution Myth*.[7]

Chapter 15
Creation versus other Scientific Theories concerning Origins

GEOLOGY CLAIMS TO HAVE DISPROVED THE BIBLE

When a girl relayed to her mother what the children's club evangelist had said about the realities of heaven and hell, the mother complained to the club organisers. She said that she didn't mind her daughter being told "OK" Bible stories such as Noah and the Flood, but she objected to straight gospel preaching. But how could anyone describe the account of the destruction of the earth and the total wipe-out of mankind (except for the eight saved in the Ark) as OK? Only because the mother had been taught that the Flood was a myth and not a serious truth of Scripture. This is the direct result of the principle of uniformitarianism, first proposed in the study of geology over two centuries ago. Uniformitarianism is the claim that the natural processes now operating are alone sufficient to account for the development of the natural world in past ages; and it was early adopted by Darwin when he extrapolated the theory of macro-evolution from observation of the ("micro-evolutionary") differences between finches' beaks on different islands of the Galapagos in the 1830s. And yet the fossil record rather points to catastrophism and rapid burial processes, which are more in line with the Flood account in Genesis 6-8, than to the ideas of slow deposition over millions of years. Modern geology has somewhat reluctantly reverted to including catastrophic explanations. And after the Indian-ocean tsunami of Boxing Day 2007, Japan's tsunami of 2011 that caused the Fukushima nuclear disaster, and recent UK severe weather with its accompanying flooding events, we know for certain that catastrophes do happen! Despite this, uniformitarianism still dominates scientific thinking, and the Flood is still treated as a myth. Sadly, this results in people accepting the word of scientists rather than the word of God. As a consequence they conveniently ignore the gospel warnings found in 2 Peter 2:4-9 & 3:3-9. But, as believers, we trust the plain truth of Scripture. As the Lord Jesus Himself said, "Scripture cannot be broken" (John 10:35); and, to His Father, "Your word is truth" (17:17).

PHYSICS CLAIMS THAT THE UNIVERSE WAS FORMED BY A 'BIG BANG'!

This theory is now science's predominant answer to the question of the origin of the universe (although all the explosions I have encountered as a chemist have caused chaos, not order!). By extrapolating data gleaned from present-day observations of the universe cosmologists suggest that it did actually have a beginning – in the "Big Bang". "According to Oxford University's Professor Roger Penrose, the probability of the big bang producing a universe like ours by chance (that is with the required state of order) is around 1 divided by $[10^{10}]^{23}$. This probability is so low it cannot be adequately described."[1] No wonder that cosmologists can only offer theoretical explanations for how the universe could have expanded from the original concentrated matter! And their theory can never account for how matter was *initially created*, the crucial point in the quotation from Dr. Colin Curry[2] cited in Chapter 13. No wonder, too, that the man in the street thinks the whole idea of a big bang is ludicrous!

Authoritatively, Genesis 1:1 declares, "In the beginning God created the heavens and the earth"! Verses 14-19 then describe how the universe[3], that is, extra-terrestrial space, was established on the fourth day of creation. Although earth with its atmosphere is the focus of these verses of Genesis 1, several times the Old Testament states that God "stretched out the heavens"[4] – "like a curtain and spreads them like a tent to dwell in" (Isaiah 40:22 & 45:12, 18). God has positioned the earth within the universe, "He...hangs the earth on nothing" (Job 26:7). God created our universe through His Son, who upholds it "by the word of his power" (Hebrews 1:3). The Son created all things and continues to hold everything together (compare Colossians 1:17).

The Anthropic principle[5] stands in direct contrast to the unproven 'Big Bang' hypothesis. It raises the fundamental question "Why?" again. "Why is the universe so finely tuned for human life upon earth?" The Anthropic principle[5] is the self-evident principle, discovered by physicists, that all constants of the universe such as the correct distance of the earth from the sun and its near perfect circular orbit around it, the size of the earth and its atmosphere, its tilt, the force of gravity, etc., are precisely those necessary to sustain intelligent life and especially mankind. It is one which is conveniently forgotten or brushed aside by scientists because it points unmistakably to the Creator! As Isaiah 45:18 (NKJV) confirms, "For thus says the LORD, Who created the heavens, Who is God, Who formed the earth and made it, Who has established it, Who did not create it in vain, *Who formed it to be inhabited*: 'I am the LORD, and there is no other'" (my emphasis).

MIND THE GAP!

I have to include the "Gap theory" in this Chapter because it was accepted, albeit uncritically, and taught by many nineteenth-century evangelicals – including some Brethren forefathers (and it is still held by some Brethren today). Known also as the "Ruin-Restoration" theory, and upheld in the Scofield Reference Bible,[6] it admits geological and associated paleontological scientific teachings.[7] Thomas Chambers[8] developed the "Gap Theory" to counteract the challenge of uniformitarianism by postulating a "gap of many ages of time" in between Genesis 1:1 and 1:2, whilst remaining true to the literal six days of creation, and resolutely opposing evolutionism.

But there cannot be such a gap:

1 The Sabbath laws are founded upon the one-week timescale – the fact that the Lord worked for six days to make heaven and earth, the sea, and all that is in them, then rested on the seventh day (Exodus 20:8-11 & 31:17, repeated in Deuteronomy 5:12-15). Therefore, His initial work, the creation of the universe from nothing (Romans 4:17 & Hebrews 11:3), is part of Day One, a fact that is clearly stated in Genesis 2:1-4. He asked Israel to obey this rule: six days of activity and one day's rest (that is, a *weekly* cycle of life), which He himself had established by His own example.

2 A fundamental truth of the gospel is that it was Adam's sin which brought death into the world (Romans 5:12). There was neither suffering nor death in the whole of creation until after the Fall/Curse (compare Genesis 2:16-17 with chapter 3). 1 Corinthians 15:45 states that Adam was the first man – ever! "By a man came death" in verse 21 therefore means "by Adam", who was not created until Day Six (Genesis 1:27).

3 Isaiah 45:18 clearly says that God did not leave the earth in a state of suspended emptiness. Genesis 1:2 records the immediate action of the Spirit of God upon the waters. Thereafter God formed the earth to be inhabited by mankind during Days Two, Three, Five, and Six.

4 Birds, fish, animals, etc., were not created until Days Five and Six, so fossils could not have been formed earlier than that. The mass destruction of animal life during the Flood is sufficient to account for the fossil record.

5 The Lord Jesus Christ connected Genesis 1:1 with 1:27 when He said in Mark 10:6 concerning marriage, "from the beginning of creation (i.e., Genesis 1:1), 'God made them male and female.'" He also said in Luke 11:50 that mankind existed "from the foundation of the world," again showing that Genesis 1:1 & 1:27 were concurrent in time (that is, occurred in the same week).

A variation of the Gap theory was the Day-Age theory, that is, that geological epochs somehow can be mapped on to the creation "days", which are viewed as figurative expressions. This can be readily dismissed by the recurrent statement "there was evening and morning, an xth day" (Genesis 1:5, 8, 13, 19, 23 & 31) and the explanation of the Sabbath in the Decalogue in (1) above.

Chapter 16
On Whose Authority?

"SCIENCE" CLAIMS TO HAVE PROVED THAT GOD DOES NOT EXIST

The combined current scientific views on origins advanced by evolutionists, geologists, cosmologists and other scientists provide militant atheists and aggressive secular materialists with a "scientific" basis for claiming, "There is *probably* no God!" This slogan was used in a humanist advertising campaign on London buses a few years ago. The Psalmist has an answer for such statements. "The fool says in his heart, 'There is no God'" (Psalm 14:1, repeated 53:1). The Psalmist is not calling such persons fools for *thinking* there is no God, but for *telling* themselves there is no God, because deep down in their minds they know the reality is that God does exist! The unbeliever does not disbelieve: he *rejects* – "in his heart", and in the Bible the "heart" of man means his *will*. Though they will strenuously deny it, the fact is that "his invisible attributes, namely, his eternal power and divine nature, have been clearly perceived, ever since the creation of the world, in the things that have been made. So they are without excuse" (Romans 1:20).

"The things that are made" translates a single Greek word, *poiēma*, which is translated "workmanship" in Ephesians 2:10. When any person honestly examines the universe, or the human body in its still-unfathomed complexity, Romans 1:20 says he/she must conclude they are God's handiwork – bear His signature, that is, he/she must conclude that He exists. Psalm 19:1-6 state that creation shouts out the glory of God. Romans 1:20 reaches the emphatic conclusion that to ignore the truth of the Creator leaves a person without "a rag of excuse"! (J. B. Phillips paraphrase). Romans 1:25 teaches that it is also to deliberately believe the lie (NKJV) that God was not the Creator of the universe and the Originator of life.

But God has also revealed Himself through His word (compare Psalm 19:7-11). God told Moses His name, "I AM WHO I AM", which basically means "the One who is" (Exodus 3:14, Septuagint). This finds its echo is each person's conscience, for the Bible asserts, "[God] has put eternity in [people's] hearts, except that no one can find out the work that God does from beginning to end" (Ecclesiastes 3:11, NKJV).

THE CRUCIAL QUESTION "WHY?"

Science, at best, can answer "How?" and "What?" It can *never* answer the key question, "Why?" We know this from experience in bringing up children – their questions always end up with, "Why?"!

Here is an example of what I mean from my professional career in the chemical industry. In May 1974, I investigated a problem batch of a compound. The Quality Control analysis gave an assay of 0%! In other words, we had not manufactured the intended product. With the help of Newcastle University, I confirmed that this was indeed the case; the product was a different compound to the intended compound. From the University report, the R&D chemists deduced that the wrong catalyst had been used in the manufacturing process. But the question remained, "Why did it happen?" Later in 1974 I discovered the answer. The batch processing took place on Saturday 04 May 1974, the day that Newcastle United played Liverpool in the F.A. Cup final at Wembley. The process Operator belatedly admitted that he had not checked the identity of the catalyst charged because he was anxious to get back to the tea room to continue watching the match on the television. And to cap it all, for both of us, Newcastle United lost! Only he could reveal the answer – there was no scientific way I could have ever discovered it!

Returning to the question "Why?", it must be expanded to "Why should anything exist, rather than nothing at all?" The scientist may rightly rule such a question out of order as non-scientific; but he or she thereby rules him(her)self out, as a scientist, from making statements regarding the origin of the universe and the existence of God. But such questions must have *some* answer. All science is limited in scope to the natural and material universe. The Bible declares that "God is spirit" (John 4:24), therefore He cannot be discovered by scientific investigation. Job 11:7 (KJV) asks, "Canst thou by searching find out God? Canst thou find out the Almighty unto perfection [His limits, NKJV]?" But because *God* took the initiative, rather than man's "searching" having the initiative, He can, and has, made nature the evidence of His own Being, as we have seen in Romans 1:20. And, so that we can know Him personally, God has chosen to reveal Himself to mankind through His word (compare Psalm 19:7-14); but supremely through His Son, the Word (John 1:1-4, 14 & 18). *Christ is the complete answer to the question "Why?"* All things have been created by Him and for Him (Colossians 1:16-17 with John 1:1-3, N.Tr.).

CONCLUSION: THE AUTHORITY OF SCRIPTURE

As with all matters of life and faith, so also for teaching about Creation and the Creator: Christian believers stand by the authority of Scripture. We should always ask, "What do the Scriptures actually say about the issue?" Compare Luke 10:26, Romans 4:3 and Galatians 4:30. We must continue to insist that God is always true (Romans 3:4). To the Corinthians Paul three times wrote that God is absolutely true to His word, "God is faithful" (1 Corinthians 1:9, 10:13 & 2 Corinthians 1:18). And, for myself, I have always lived by the axiom to believe Scripture even when the scientific teaching appears to be to the contrary! As Psalm 119:160 (KJV) asserts, "Thy word is true from the beginning: and every one of thy righteous judgments endureth for ever." For example, if Thomas Chambers and others had stood by this principle there would be no "Gap Theory" (see Chapter 15). Historically, Christians had always accepted that Day One was described by Genesis 1:1-3; and that the universe was only a few thousand years old until the theory of uniformitarianism was postulated. And it was postulated with the intent of discrediting the Bible record of the Flood! As 2 Peter 3:3-4 predicted, "scoffers will come in the last days ... [saying] '... all things are continuing as they were from the beginning of creation.'"

GOSPEL APPEAL

If you are not a believer, and have reached this point in the book, I appeal to you to acknowledge your Creator

God and believe the Gospel. As this is the conclusion of the 'science' part of the book, I know of a 'scientific experiment' which you can do for yourself to prove (establish as fact) that the Gospel is true. I call it 'the Taste Test' for Psalm 34:8 invites everyone, "Oh, taste and see that the LORD is good! Blessed is the man who takes refuge in him!" (In the early part of my career as an analytical chemist, I actually performed taste tests, but these are now prohibited by health & safety rules.) But the "taste and see that the LORD is good" is not restricted to scientific professionals, for Jesus said He will receive whoever comes to Him (John 6:37). However, there are two control conditions, as we would say in the trade, you must apply:

1 *Faith*. Hebrews 11:6 says you need to have faith that God exists and that He rewards those who seek Him. I suggest you read Job 38-41 to find out about Him, the Creator, and be humbled before Him.

2 *Repentance*. You must understand how far short of His standards you have fallen and admit this to Him. You must therefore repent of your sins and place your faith for salvation in the Lord Jesus Christ, who died for your sins and rose again. I suggest you read Romans 1-5 & 10 to get a good understanding of the doctrines of the Christian Gospel.

By carrying out the 'Taste Test' in this way, you are definitely assured of a positive result, for the Bible says, "The same Lord is Lord of all, bestowing his riches on all who call on him. For everyone who calls on the name of the Lord will be saved" (Romans 10:12-13). The Gospel of the grace of God is "repentance towards God and … faith in our Lord Jesus Christ" (Acts 20:21).

BENEDICTION AND DOXOLOGY

I finish my book on creation with a Scriptural benediction from the Creator, one which closes with a
doxology to Him. It is Psalm 115:13-18,

"[The LORD (that is, the Creator, see verse 15)] will bless
those who fear [him], both the small and the great. May
the LORD give you increase, you and your children! May
you be blessed by the LORD, who made heaven and
earth! The heavens are the LORD's heavens, but the earth
he has given to the children of man. The dead do not
praise the LORD, nor do any who go down into silence.
But we will bless the LORD from this time forth and
forevermore. Praise the LORD!"

Notes

NOTES ON PART 1 — THE FUNDAMENTALS

NOTE ON CHAPTER 1

[1] Compare Genesis 1:20-21, 24 & 30; 2:7 & 19.

NOTES ON CHAPTER 2

[1] Compare Isaiah 29:16 & 64:8; Jeremiah 18:3-4 & 6.

[2] "Empty" means "without form" in Genesis 1:2.

[3] *God always works towards the day*. For example, the millennial day (2 Samuel 23:4 & Revelation 21:25); the resurrection day (Psalm 22 title); and the day of eternity (2 Peter 3:18, also N.Tr.).

[4] Robert Young, *A Literal Translation of the Holy Bible*. (G. A. Young & Co, 1898).
N.Tr. translates "day one" as "the first day."

[5] Genesis 5:1; 6:9; 10:1; 11:10; 11:27; 25:12, 19; 36:1, 9; 37:2.

[6] See Vine, W. E., Unger, M. F., & White, W. *Vine's complete expository dictionary of Old and New Testament words*. (Nashville, Tennessee, Thomas Nelson Publishers, 1996).

NOTES ON CHAPTER 3

[1] 1 Corinthians 15:47 with 2 Corinthians 5:21, 1 Peter 2:22 & 1 John 3:5.

[2] A.H. is *Anno Hominis*, "in the year of man".

[3] 2 Peter 3: 5-7 (ASV).

[4] Genesis 2:4; 5:1; 6:9; 10:1; 11:10; 11:27; 25:12; 25:19; 36:1 & 9; 37:2.

NOTES ON PART 2 — BIBLICAL TEACHING ABOUT CREATION

NOTES ON CHAPTER 4

[1] See, for example, Mark 3:1-5 & John 5:1-18.

[2] See the exposition of Hebrews 11:3 in W.E. Vine, "Hebrews", reprinted in *The Collected Writings of W.E. Vine* (Nashville, Tennessee, Thomas Nelson Publishers, 5-volume set, 1996), Volume 3.

[3] Genesis 1:3, 6, 9, 11, 14, 20, 24, 26 & Psalm 33:6-9.

[4] Genesis 6-8.

[5] Also: Isaiah 13:6 & 9; Jeremiah 46:10; Ezekiel 13:5 & 30:3; Joel 1:15, 2:1, 11 & 31, 3:14; Amos 5:18 & 20; Obadiah 1:15; Zephaniah 1:7, 8 & 14; Malachi 4:5; Acts 2:20; 1 Corinthians 5:5; 1 Thessalonians 5:2 & 2 Thessalonians 2:2.

[6] See, for example, Isaiah 24:19-20 & Zechariah 14:4.

[7] Psalm 8:6-8 shows the extent of Adam's dominion.

[8] See Chapter 10.

[9] See Chapter 12 and 2 Corinthians 5:17; Colossians 1:18; Revelation 3:14.

NOTES ON CHAPTER 5

[1] With the advent of super resolution microscopes, scientists have discovered the 'simple cell' to be as complex as a fully-functioning factory!

[2] James G. Deck, *Hymns and Sacred Poems* (London, Broom & Rouse, 1889), page 1.

[3] Genesis 1:3, 6, 9, 11, 14, 20, 24 with 1:26 (KJV) and confirmed by Psalm 33:6 & 9, Psalm 148:5, with Hebrews 11:3.

[4] Psalm 119:90; Jeremiah 10:12, 51:15; Proverbs 3:19, 8:27.

[5] Job 9:8; Isaiah 40:22, 42:5, 44:24, 45:12 & 51:13; Jeremiah 10:12 & 51:15; Zechariah 12:1.

[6] Psalm 102:25; Job 38:4; Isaiah 48:13; Hebrews 1:10. See also "the foundations of the earth" in Psalm 82:5; Psalm 104:5; Proverbs 8:29; Isaiah 24:18, 40:21, 51:13 & 16; Jeremiah 31:37; Micah 6:2.

[7] Matthew 13:35 & 25:34; Luke 11:50; Hebrews 4:3 & 9:26; Revelation 17:8.

[8] John 17:24; Ephesians 1:4; 1 Peter 1:20; Revelation 13:8 (compare "before times eternal", 2 Timothy 1:9 (ASV)).

[9] Other references: 1 Chronicles 16:30; Proverbs 30:4; Jeremiah 10:12 & 51:15.

[10] Exodus 6:6; Deuteronomy 4:34, 5:15, 7:19, 9:29, 11:2 & 26:8; 1 Kings 8:42; 2 Kings 17:36; 2 Chronicles 6:32; Psalm 136:12; Jeremiah 32:21; Ezekiel 20:33-34.

[11] This is an example of the 'Anthropic principle', that is, that so many features of the universe, if they were only a tiny bit different from what they are, would make life

(especially human life) on earth impossible. See Chapter 15, note 5.

[12] A light year (l.y.) = 9.461 x 10^{15} metres.

[13] Stuart Burgess, *He Made the Stars Also* (Leominster, Day One Publications, 2001), page 81.

NOTES ON PART 3 — CREATION IN THE OLD TESTAMENT

NOTES ON CHAPTER 6

[1] *New and Concise Bible Dictionary* (London, G. Morrish, 1897-1900).

[2] Behemoth was a dinosaur, that is, a land reptile. Leviathan was a sea-dragon, mentioned again in Psalm 74:14, Psalm 104:26 & Isaiah 27:1. Rahab was some kind of dragon, mentioned again in Psalm 87:4, Psalm 89:10 and Isaiah 30:7 & 51:9.

[3] I was an analytical chemist in the 1970s. In those days we used 'balance brushes' to clean the pans in order to zero the analytical balances. So fine was the dust, it could not been seen with the naked eye. (Nowadays, self-adjusting electronic scales are in vogue.)

[4] Also, 46:4, 48:12, 51:12, 52:6, N.Tr. (See Chapter 8 comments and note on Psalm 102:27.)

[5] Also, 40:22, 26 & 28; 42:5; 44:24; 45:7-8, 12 & 18; 48:13; 51:13.

[6] *Bara*, as in Genesis 1:1.

[7] *Yâtsar*, as in Genesis 2:7.

[8] Romans 11:26.

[9] *Asah*, as in Genesis 1:7, 16, 25-26 & 31; 2:2-4 & 18.

[10] W. E. Vine, *The Collected Writings of W. E. Vine* (Nashville, Tennessee, Thomas Nelson Publishers, 5-volume set, 1996) Volume 1, page 121.

[11] These ideas occur in other prophecies. For example, Ezekiel 47:1-12; Joel 2:10 & 30-31; Amos 9:13-14; Micah 4:1 and Zechariah 14:3-9.

[12] See Chapter 10, 'Creation Restored'.

NOTES ON PART 4 — CREATION IN THE PSALMS

NOTES ON OVERVIEW

[1] In addition to Psalms discussed in Chapters 7-9, other Psalms extolling the creatorial greatness of Israel's covenant God include Psalms 46; 111:5b-9; 66:5-7; 68:7-10 & 28-35; 74:12-17; 78:12-16, 23-29 & 42-55; 105:12-16 & 26-41; 106:8-11; 115:12-18; 135:4-12; and Psalm 136.

[2] In addition to Psalms discussed in Chapters 7-9, see also Psalm 89:3-29 & 35-37; and Psalms 93, 96-98.

NOTES ON CHAPTER 7

[1] Tom Summerhill, 'Some observations on Psalm 8', *Grace & Truth Magazine*, *www.gtpress.org*, May 2009, pages 13-17.

[2] For further expositions of Psalm 8 see:

> a. Chapter 11, 'Christ, the Son of Man set over all Creation'.

> b. Two other published articles in *Grace & Truth Magazine*, May 2009:

>> i. 'God's Glory In Creation', David R Reid, pages 3-5.

    ii. 'The Significance of Man In The Universe', Doug Hayhoe, pages 8-12.

  c. 'The Son of Man', Yannick Ford, *Scripture Truth* magazine, October 2007.

[3] Or "voice" (ESV footnote). N.Tr. footnote explains: "[line,] that is, the 'extent' of their testimony."

[4] See also Psalms 96:5; 115:15; 124:8; 134:3; 146:6.

[5] Translated by Stuart K. Hine. Copyright © 1953 *Stuart K. Hine/Kingsway's Thankyou Music.*

[6] Genesis 1:3, 6-7, 9, 11, 14-15, 20, 24 & 26.

[7] See also Psalms 104:27-29; 107:23-31 & 35-38; 135:5-7; 136:4-9; 145:15-17; 147:15-18.

[8] Derek Kidner, *Psalms 1-72. Tyndale Old Testament Commentaries* (London, Inter-Varsity Press, 1973) page 137.

Notes on Chapter 8

[1] In the Old Testament, 'The Same' is sometimes translated 'I am HE' – see N.Tr. footnote with its references for Deuteronomy 32:39.

[2] H.L. Ellison, *The Psalms*, (London, Scripture Union, 1968), page 86.

[3] Matthew 26:36-45, Mark 14:32 & Luke 22:41-44.

[4] J.N. Darby, *Synopsis of the Bible*, (Kingston on Thames, London, Stow Hill Bible and Tract Depot, 1943), Vol. II, page 161.

[5] Also, Job 16:13 & 19:27; Psalms 7:9, 16:7, 26:2 & 73:21; Proverbs 23:16; Jeremiah 11:20, 12:2 & 20:12 and Lamentations 3:13.

[6] Christian ethical perspectives arising from these verses are detailed by:

- John Wyatt, *Matters of Life and Death*, (Leicester, IVP, 2nd Edition, 2009).
- John R Ling, *When does human life begin*, (Newcastle upon Tyne, The Christian Institute, Salt & Light Series, June 2011).

[7] LORD we are Thine, J. G. Deck (1807-84), as printed in *Hymns of Light and Love*, (Bath, Echoes of Service)

NOTES ON CHAPTER 9

[1] Revelation 11:15, with 19:1, 3, 4 & 6.

[2] J. M. Flanigan, *What the Bible Teaches – Psalms* (Kilmarnock, John Ritchie, 2001), page 617.

[3] Alphabetical Psalms are Psalms which have an acrostic formation. That is, the verses begin with letters of the Hebrew alphabet. See W. G. Scroggie, *The Psalms. Appendix II*, (London, Pickering & Inglis, reprinted 1967), page 292.

[4] This assumes acceptance of the inclusion of verse 13b, i.e., the Hebrew letter *Nūn*, as in the Septuagint version.

[5] High points are always reached in Israel's history and worship when they remember Jehovah's steadfast love, or loving kindness – His character as revealed to Moses when he requested to see Jehovah's glory. Compare Exodus 33:18-19 & 34:6-7 with 1 Chronicles 16:34 & 41; 2 Chronicles 5:13; 6:12-14; 7:1-3 & 6; 20:21; Ezra 3:11; Psalms 106, 107, 118 & 136; Jeremiah 33:11.

[6] In Psalm 145:13, the term "everlasting kingdom, which endures throughout all generations", means that the Lord's kingdom will continue, never to be superseded, until the end of time (compare Daniel 2.44); and then it

will be delivered up to God the Father (1 Corinthians 15:24) – see also Chapter 12.

[7] G. Gilpin.

[8] W. G. Scroggie, *The Psalms. Volume Three* (London, Pickering & Inglis, reprinted 1967), page 143.

[9] J. N. Darby, *Synopsis of the Bible*, (Kingston on Thames, London, Stow Hill Bible and Tract Depot, 1943), Vol. II, p.185.

[10] See also Psalms 33:3, 40:3, 96:1, 98:1 & 144:9.

[11] Derek Kidner, *Psalms 73-150, Tyndale Old Testament Commentaries*, (London, Inter-Varsity Press, 1973), page 491.

[12] Compare Genesis 1:20-21.

[13] Derek Kidner, page 492.

NOTE ON CONCLUSION

[1] Sir Edward Denny (1796-1889).

NOTES ON PART 5 — CREATION TO COME

NOTES ON CHAPTER 11

[1] In verse 4 the first "man" translates the Hebrew enosh (man in his frailty), whilst "son of man" is "son of Adam", speaking of man in his dignity.

[2] See Chapter 5, note 11 & Chapter 15, note 5.

[3] See note 1.

[4] Or "the heavenly Man," NKJV – "man out of heaven," verse 47 (N.Tr.).

[5] J. G. Deck (1807-84).

NOTES ON CHAPTER 12

[1] F. B. Hole, *The Great Salvation* (London, 1937), page 115.

[2] For the figure of speech, compare Jeremiah 49:23.

[3] For example, "pangs of death" in Acts 2:24. Joseph Henry Thayer's *Greek-English Lexicon of the New Testament* renders "birth pangs" as the literal meaning of the Greek word for pangs. [Thayer Definition: 1) the pain of childbirth, travail pain, birth pangs].

NOTES ON PART 6 — CREATION POSTSCRIPT

NOTES ON CHAPTER 13

[1] Colin Curry, *The Heart of Christianity*, (Central Bible Hammond Trust Ltd, Wooler, 1989), pages 17-18.

[2] Chirality concerns mirror-image chemicals, or left-handed and right-handed chemicals.

[3] Technically,

> a. peptides are short polymers of amino acids, with up to 50 monomers

> b. polypeptides are polymers of 10-100 amino acids

> c. an oligonucleotide is a nucleic acid polymer, typically with more than 50 bases.

[4] See, David Rosevear, *The Myth of Chemical Evolution*, (Institute for Creation Research, 1999, www.icr.org/article/49/281).

NOTES ON CHAPTER 14

[1] The correct terminology is "gas evolution". Unwittingly, the teacher referred to a fact already known in Proverbs 25:20.

[2] Edgar Andrews, *Who made God?* (Darlington, Evangelical Press, 2009), page 215, with my emphasis.

[3] Creation scientists also use the methodology that "the key to the past is the present", but start from Scripture to interpret the data.

[4] John C. Lennox, *God's Undertaker. Has Science Buried God?* (Oxford, Lion, 2009), pages 109-110. (John C. Lennox is Professor in Mathematics at the University of Oxford and Fellow in Mathematics and the Philosophy of Science at Green Templeton College.)

[5] W. E. Vine, *The Collected Writings of W. E. Vine*, (Nashville, Tennessee, Thomas Nelson Publishers, 5-volume set, 1996), Volume 2, pages 89-90.

[6] John C. Lennox, *God's Undertaker. Has Science Buried God?* (Oxford, Lion, 2009), page 129.

[7] Vij Sodera, *One Small Speck to Man: the Evolution Myth*, (Bognor Regis, 2nd edition, 2009), page 8, Sodera's emphases. (*www.onesmallspeck.com*).

NOTES ON CHAPTER 15

[1] Dominic Statham, *Back to the Beginning*, (www.creation.com, 01 March 2014), Reference 4, Moreland, J. P. and Craig, W. L., *Philosophical Foundations for a Christian Worldview*, (Intervarsity Press, USA, 2003), page 483.

[2] Dr. Colin Curry was a former editor of *Scripture Truth* magazine and a senior lecturer in the Department of Physics at Leeds University.

[3] Although there is no Hebrew word for universe, the idea is represented by the phrase "the heavens and the earth": see Genesis 1:1; Deuteronomy 10:14; Nehemiah 9:6, etc.

[4] Job 9:8; Isaiah 40:22, 44:24, 45:12, 51:13; Jeremiah 10:12, 51:15; Zechariah 12:1.

[5] See Pamphlet 355, *The Anthropic Principle*, Dr. David Rosevear, (Creation Science Movement, Portsmouth, UK, March 2005).

[6] See footnote 2, on Genesis 1:1, in *The Scofield Reference Bible* (New York, Oxford University Press, 1917).

[7] Geology is the scientific study of solid earth (its rocks, strata, etc.) and the processes by which they form/change. Paleontology (palaeontology) is the scientific study of supposed "prehistoric life", especially of fossils. They are interdependent with respect to assigning dates – the age of fossils is determined by their place in the "geological column", whilst the age of strata is determined by the fossils they contain!

[8] Thomas Chambers (1780-1847) was a leading evangelical minister and theologian in the Church of Scotland, and after 1843 in the Free Church of Scotland.

About the Author

David Anderson lives in Newcastle on Tyne, where he is an active member of the assembly meeting in Edgefield Gospel Hall. He is married to Gillian and they have four adult children. For many years he was involved in organising children's summer camps at Fenham Farm, Northumberland. He is currently involved in preaching and teaching amongst UK assemblies; and at conferences. He is a regular contributor to Christian magazines and is a member of the Truth for Today broadcasts' team. Since his retirement from industry in 1998, he has been a tutor for both UK and overseas students engaged in Emmaus Bible School correspondence courses.

David worked in the Active Pharmaceutical Ingredients sector of the chemical industry for over 40 years: first, as an analytical chemist; then in quality management; and finally, as a pharmaceutical consultant until 2010.

Other Books from Scripture Truth Publications

UNDERSTANDING THE OLD TESTAMENT SERIES:

LESSONS FROM EZRA BY TED MURRAY

ISBN: 978-0-901860-75-0 (paperback)
84 pages; March 2007

LESSONS FROM NEHEMIAH BY TED MURRAY

ISBN: 978-0-901860-86-6 (paperback)
124 pages; August 2008

THE GOSPEL IN JOB BY YANNICK FORD

ISBN: 978-0-901860-76-7 (paperback)
ISBN: 978-0-901860-77-4 (hardback)
112 pages; March 2007

PSALM 119: A COMMENTARY ON THE ENTIRE PSALM BY COR BRUINS

ISBN: 978-0-901860-88-0 (paperback)
186 pages; March 2010

CHRIST IS MY BELOVED BY GEORGE STEVENS

ISBN: 978-0-901860-84-2 (paperback)
200 pages; October 2009

UNDERSTANDING THE NEW TESTAMENT SERIES:

JESUS - A TRUE STORY BY RUTH KEABLE

ISBN: 978-0-901860-41-5 (paperback)
108 pages; December 2006

PATMOS SPEAKS TODAY BY JOHN WESTON

ISBN: 978-0-901860-66-8 (paperback)
88 pages; February 2007

TRUTH FOR TODAY SERIES:

WHAT A GOD WE CHRISTIANS HAVE! BY GLENN BAXTER

ISBN: 978-0-0901860-59-0 (paperback)
208 pages; July 2011

UNDERSTANDING CHRISTIANITY SERIES:

GOD AND RELATIONSHIPS BY COR BRUINS

ISBN: 978-0-901860-36-1 (paperback)
108 pages; August 2006

THE TRANSFORMING POWER OF FORGIVENESS BY PHILIP NUNN

ISBN: 978-0-901860-91-0 (paperback)
90 pages; January 2012

www.ingramcontent.com/pod-product-compliance
Lightning Source LLC
LaVergne TN
LVHW051735080426
835511LV00018B/3080